Mending Hurts

Swarthmore Lecture 1987

MENDING HURTS

by
John Lampen

QUAKER HOME SERVICE · LONDON

First published May 1987
Reprinted October 1987

ISBN 0 85245 206 3

Cover design by John Lampen
The photograph by Donald Cooper of Donald
Sinden as King Lear and Tony Church as Gloster is
from the Royal Shakespeare Company's 1976
production and is reproduced by permission of the
Shakespeare Centre Library, Stratford-upon-Avon.
Back cover photo by Frank Lampen

Printed in 11/13pt Palatino by Headley Brothers Ltd.,
The Invicta Press, Ashford, Kent and London

Preface

The Swarthmore Lectureship was established by the Woodbrooke Extension Committee at a meeting held December 9th, 1907: the minute of the Committee providing for 'an annual lecture on some subject relating to the message and work of the Society of Friends'. The name Swarthmore was chosen in memory of the home of Margaret Fell, which was always open to the earnest seeker after Truth, and from which loving words of sympathy and substantial material help were sent to her co-workers.

The lectureship has a twofold purpose: first, to interpret further to the members of the Society of Friends their message and mission; and, second, to bring before the public the spirit, the aims and fundamental principles of Friends. The lecturer alone is responsible for any opinions expressed.

The lectureship provides both for the publication of a book and for a delivery of a lecture, the latter usually at the time of assembly of London Yearly Meeting of the Society of Friends. A lecture related to the present book was delivered at Friends House, Euston Road, London, on the evening of Saturday, May 23, 1987.

Contents

Lear: No, no! Come, let's away to prison:
We two alone will sing like birds i'th' cage:
When thou dost ask me blessing, I'll kneel
    down
And ask of thee forgiveness: so we'll live,
And pray, and sing, and tell old tales, and
    laugh
At gilded butterflies, and hear poor rogues
Talk of court news; and we'll talk with them
    too,
Who loses and who wins, who's in, who's out,
And take upon 's the mystery of things
As if we were God's spies; and we'll wear out,
In a walled prison, packs and sects of great
    ones
That ebb and flow by the moon.

Edmund: Take them away.

Lear: Upon such sacrifices, my Cordelia,
The gods themselves throw incense.

        William Shakespeare: *King Lear*, Act V scene 3.

Introduction

I would like to dedicate this book to the memory of my father.

I have tried to draw on experience in this book. As I worked I became aware of many other writers who shed light, sometimes obliquely, on what I wanted to say. Quotations from them appear, as it were in the margin, on the left hand pages of this book. Where the source is a Quaker one, I have indicated this with a Q. The right hand pages therefore give the text of the Swarthmore Lecture as it was delivered, and the two songs formed part of the lecture.

I would like to thank those who allowed me to quote them, and apologise for any unintentional breaches of copyright. Specific acknowledgements are given at the end of the book. I owe a great deal to those who helped me to clarify my thought, specially my wife Diana, Jo Farrow, Rabbi David Rosen, Sister Mary Grant and the members of the Swarthmore Lecture Committee. Clifford Barnard and Melvyn Rose gave me invaluable technical help. Friends House Library staff followed up many references for me. Most of all I must thank all those who, at Shotton Hall, in Northern Ireland and elsewhere, shared with me in the experiences on which the book is based.

John Lampen

SOURCES OF PAIN

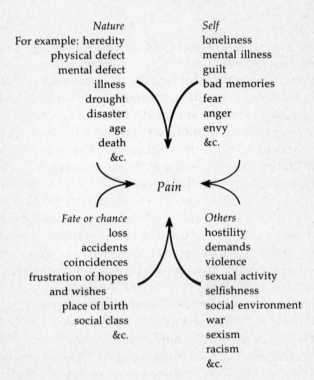

Nature
For example: heredity
physical defect
mental defect
illness
drought
disaster
age
death
&c.

Self
loneliness
mental illness
guilt
bad memories
fear
anger
envy
&c.

Pain

Fate or chance
loss
accidents
coincidences
frustration of hopes
and wishes
place of birth
social class
&c.

Others
hostility
demands
violence
sexual activity
selfishness
social environment
war
sexism
racism
&c.

Pain and Hurt

Most of us do not find it easy to manage pain. We do not like to think about it, or watch it in others. And when it strikes us, we seek ways to be quickly rid of it. Even with physical pain, we do not see any good reason to tolerate it, when we are offered an armoury of analgesics; and we feel somehow cheated when the doctor says he cannot help. When the pain is in the heart and mind, we look for other kinds of strategy, just as sure that it is our right to be at peace within ourselves. The old idea that the world is a vale of tears strikes us as not merely wrong-headed but destructive; we can see how it was used to oppress the destitute.

There are four sources of pain: there is ourselves, other people, the natural world, and chance, or fate, or (as many would say) God. These distinctions are of course not clear-cut; they merge into each other. Our own desires and bad memories cause us pain, our envy, anger, fear and guilt, our loneliness. We are hurt by the misunderstanding and hostility of others, and their selfishness and demands (physical, sexual and emotional), and at times by their cruelty. It can hurt to

Machine gunners have me in their sights
               there is barbed wire around me
               electrified wire
I am on a list
I am called all day
They have tatooed me
               and marked me with a number
They have photographed me behind the barbed wire
All my bones can be counted
               as on an X-ray film
They have stripped me of my identity
They have led me naked to the gas-chamber
They have shared out my clothes and my shoes
               Ernesto Cardenal: part of *Psalm 22*

Suffering is difficult to define. Basically it is something (maybe quite minor) which happens against our will, is unpleasant, and blows our carefully-regulated lives asunder. We protest, kicking and screaming for the restoration of the *status quo ante*. If we can persuade ourselves to stop struggling and come to terms with the pain, adapt our natural rhythms to it, accept it as no better and no worse than it is, we may still be floundering in darkness, but the darkness may contain the promise of light.
               Mary Craig: *Blessings*, p.126

2

love them and to lose them. They create the social environment which may bear heavily on us, through indifference, expectation, exploitation, injustice and war. The natural world may harm us through its heat, cold and drought, through flood and earthquake; but also through the laws of heredity, through physical or mental defect, through illness and death. And what we can call providence or chance, the 'givenness' of life, brings the circumstances of our inheritance and situation, painful accidents and coincidences, and the frustration of many of our hopes and wishes.

The sadness which stems from nature or fate may be very deep; but most of us find resources for coming to terms with it. This may not happen at once—I remember a clergyman telling a teenage girl that her father's early death was God's will, and she replied hotly, 'Then you can keep your God!' But it is possible for most of us to acknowledge our common mortality, our liability to sickness, accident and bereavement, and to renounce any wish for special privileges. To be free of the suffering which we cause one another (and consequently ourselves), individually and in groups, is more difficult and costly. It is this kind of pain, often mental pain, which I shall speak of as 'hurt'. Our ability to tolerate it, or rather to work our passage through it, varies widely. My friend Eileen had three small children and was pregnant when she last saw her husband, with a hood over his head, being taken out of the house by two masked men with guns. He was later found dead in the street. I cannot explain why she looks to the future with tough-minded

I was a hitter. I couldn't express myself and I hit. I fought men and I hit women. That is why I am always on about love and peace, you see. It's the most violent people who go for love and peace. Everything's the opposite. But I sincerely believe in love and peace. I am a violent man who has learnt not to be violent and regrets his violence. I will have to be a lot older before I can face in public how I treated women as a youngster.

> John Lennon in *The Playboy Interviews*
> by David Sheff, p.154

... I
who've followed so many times
the path from killer to victim
from victim to punishment
from punishment to the next murder,
groping ...

> George Seferis: *Gymnopaedia*

4

optimism and laughter, while Mary, whose life seems to have been so even and her troubles so ordinary, is crushed by chronic depression.

Pain has been described as the one form of evil which we cannot remember after it has passed. But this clearly refers to physical pain. We know how the hurt in the heart persists, and can be recalled at will and often against our will. When we hurt ourselves, whether from bad memories, guilt, fear or resentment, we can usually trace this back to suffering inflicted by others, maybe long ago. But we are not always conscious of these unhealed wounds. When their pain threatens to become acute, habits of defence assert themselves to protect us.

One way in which we try to drive it out is by hurting someone else. I seem to have a magical belief that if I am smarting from someone's aggression towards me, I will feel better if I—as we say—'take out my feelings' on you. In uncountable instances suffering is being passed on in this way. The child who is bullied becomes a bully. The youngster who has been given nothing by his community breaks the phone in the kiosk or beats up the person he is robbing. The man who is abused at work goes home and plays the tyrant in his family. And on a larger scale, whole social groups, whole nations, look to the exercise of violence to obliterate their own sense of humiliation and exploitation. In families, neighbourhoods, institutions, industries, societies, and the whole world community, cycles of deprivation, hurt, revenge, and renewed hurt have persisted, often from so long ago

If one listens patiently to a melancholic's many and various self-accusations, one cannot in the end avoid the impression that often the most violent of them are hardly at all applicable to the patient himself, but that with insignificant modifications they do fit someone else, someone whom the patient loves or has loved or should love. So we find the key to the clinical picture: we perceive that the self-reproaches are reproaches against a loved object which have been shifted away from it on to the patient's own ego.

Sigmund Freud: *Mourning and Melancholia*, p.256

The pain was not less. Or perhaps it must have become less since he could behave normally, eat meals and go back to the office. It was as if the pain remained there but he had grown larger all round it and could contain it more easily. It no longer bent and racked his body. He carried it inside himself gently, almost gingerly, as if it were a precious egg.

Iris Murdoch: *Bruno's Dream*, p. 238

that their origins are unknown.

But many do not command the force or guile to try to pass on their hurt; or they know that doing so makes them feel guilty and so renews their pain. Instead they direct it not against other people but themselves. When I was working with emotionally damaged young people, I often saw how, if one of them inhibited his anger, the outward thrust of his pain, it turned back on him as depression. It was a cruel choice; whether to let his anger eat away at himself, his drive and will—or to let it hurt someone else, giving momentary relief until it returned to him in the form of self-reproach.

A third way in which we fail to resolve our pain, but try to make it bearable, is to seal it tightly inside ourselves, something which we can take pride in and cling to, so that we feel to give it up would leave a gap in us, a painful loss, a renewed pang sharper than the dull ache of it.

Small wonder that, given these choices, we try to avoid the source of hurt. In a world of people which offers so much opportunity for love and contact and exploration and enrichment, we recall that all these things carry with them the risk of disappointment, loss and grief; and so we step back and wall ourselves up with a few others who have learnt the way we play our game. We can dress up our self-protection with the best of excuses. Even the way in which we Quakers express our testimony for peace can bear witness to our failure to come to terms with our aggression; our insistence on 'that of God in every-

* The experience of hurt is powerfully expressed in *Lamentations, 3:1–21*.

Whenever we intercede in prayer we must be prepared for an answer which places a practical obligation upon us. A prayer is always a commitment.

Thomas Green: *Preparation for Worship*, p. 31   Q

In her lecture last year, Damaris Parker-Rhodes said a very severe thing which, to me, struck home: 'Many religious people never come to possess their inner selves, and they use their form of worship as a vaccination to keep them safe from living experience.' That living experience includes very dark places; and yet it is the revelation and examination of those dark places which people most resent in modern literature and drama, and dread to find and face in themselves.

John Ormerod Greenwood: *Signs of Life*, p. 62   Q

one' at times confesses to our refusal to admit how much others can hurt us.*

If we are to try to mend some of the hurts in the world around us, we must be able to face them. But as we allow the pain of others to reach us, we reawaken the ache of our own past wounds; and this frightens us. One way of meeting this problem may be in prayer—for others and for ourselves. But even this can be our way of protecting ourselves from feeling the real weight of someone's burden, unless we have discovered that God often answers our prayers by telling *us* to do something about the situation.

We may also enter into these experiences in imagination, through art, music and literature. When I think how often I can cry at a book or piece of music, and how seldom at direct experience, I realise how I guard my feelings in everyday encounters, and how great art can help me to descend into the depths. I urge you to remember this resource against the deadening of our sympathies which is often the paradoxical result of news coverage and discussion intended to arouse pity.

But it is clearly not enough. Literature can become a substitute for experiencing life. If any of us are serious about mending a few of the hurts in the world, we must first encounter them and participate in their pain. Even to talk to you tonight, I must remember that what I say will mean nothing unless we start together, now, with a shared feeling of intensity of the suffering we would like to ease. We may recall the amount of it, the millions of people for whom life is

We seek as people of God to be worthy vessels to deliver the Lord's transforming word, to be prophets of joy who know from experience, and can testify to the world, as George Fox did, 'that the Lord God is at work in this thick night'. Our priority is to be receptive and responsive to the life-giving Word of God, whether it comes through the written Word (the Scriptures), the incarnate Word (Jesus Christ), the corporate Word (as discerned by the gathered meeting), or the inward Word of God in our hearts which is available to each of us who seek the Truth.

This can be made easier if we face the truth within outselves, embrace the pain, and lay down our differences before God for the Holy Spirit to forgive, thus transforming us into instruments of healing.

World Gathering of Young Friends 1985: *Epistle.*   Q

Of course they called on God: but he went his way
Down among the Lost People like Dante, down
    To the stinking fosse where the injured
    Lead the ugly life of the rejected,

And showed us what evil is; not as we thought
Deeds that must be punished, but our lack of faith,
    Our dishonest mood of denial,
    The concupiscence of the oppressor.

W. H. Auden: *In memory of Sigmund Freud 1939*

pain: the thousands of children orphaned by war in Uganda, one of whom (a boy of nine, fending entirely for himself) told me how he had seen his father shot and his mother's throat cut; those who live in countries where a thought can be a crime, its punishment torture; those who could not make sense of the world we shaped for them, shut away with the files which call them 'psychotic' or pushed out again into a community which cannot understand or support them. But numbers too can be alienating; the more we call to mind, the more distant they seem to be from us. In our own country, not more than a few streets from where you or I live:

a young woman is waiting for her husband to come home; he will be drunk, and will beat her up before sexually assaulting her; and he has made her believe that his actions are entirely her fault:

a young man is in prison, who believes that doctors have implanted a radio in his brain which controls him; he was discharged from mental hospital because they felt they had no further help to offer, and he was arrested because he started screaming for help in the street:

an old man knows that he is dying, and he is terrified of death because he believes there is no forgiveness for something he did years ago; and no one will talk with him about his life and approaching death:

a little girl of four lies in the dark, listening to the

* This story is taken from a recent article on incest.

If I write any more I shall probably cry . . . which must never be done, for there is so much both personal and impersonal to cry for here that one might weep for ever and yet not shed enough tears to wipe away the pitiableness of it all.

Vera Brittain: *Testament of Youth*, p. 218
[*Part of a letter to her fiancé written in 1915*]

movements of a man in the room; in a moment he will be pulling her out of bed, and she will know from the taste of his penis whether it is her father, her uncle or her brother.*

If someone answers our 'good morning' by saying, 'Things are going badly, I've lost my job,' or by telling us about their grandmother who is dying, we feel ill at ease, we feel we must do something. When we ask how people are, we don't want an answer which calls us to action or to love and compassion. The other person has ignored the ritual reply of 'Fine, and how are you?' which does not involve us and never commits us. When someone answers us with the truth, we feel stuck, and to get unstuck we edge away . . .

Jean Vanier: *Be Not Afraid*, p. 16

When I asked Madame Eyraud why she found it necessary to let those [Jewish] refugees into her house [in occupied France], dragging after them all those dangers and problems, including the necessity of lying to the authorities, she could never fully understand what I was getting at. Her big round eyes stopped sparkling in that happy face, and she said, 'Look. Look. Who else would have taken care of them if we didn't? They needed our help and they needed it *then*.' For her . . . the spade was turned by hitting upon a deep rock; there are no deeper issues than the issue of *people needing help then*.

Philip Haillie: *Lest Innocent Blood be Shed*, p. 127

Towards Forgiveness

Comfort and cherishing

To be hurt by another, or even by ourselves, brings a sense of isolation. A wounding remark, a physical blow, carries a powerful message; but it is not easy to respond in a way which does not compound the violence. We often prefer to cut off communication, refusing to hear the deeper meaning in what has been thrown at us. In our local communities we talk of 'mindless vandalism' and 'football hooligans', in politics of 'terrorists'; and by so doing we deny that profound and terrible feelings of hurt and rejection underlie the behaviour which we are right to deplore. In our private lives too, we develop an armoury which defends us from the pain of others, specially when it takes forms which pass the hurt on to us.

Forgiveness is the medicine which can heal these hurts; but to reach the place where forgiveness can be offered and accepted may be a long hard journey. At the beginning of the task of healing, first aid is often needed. That involves each of us caring about the loneliness of pain. It means building our relationships strong enough to contain it. It means risking

15

Training for relief work should be much more in the nature of a spiritual and social experience than a period of instruction. The relief worker's job is to live adaptably and imaginatively in unforseen circumstances, maintaining inward balance in a world full of tensions and frustrations. To develop and maintain a capacity for purposeful living in the midst of degradation, a sense of confident daring is of supreme importance ... Relief work involves the whole personality and cannot be effectively done, at any rate in a Quaker setting, by those who are able to offer certain technical skills and little more. This is not to say that the heart is all-important and skills are secondary, but the skills are no use unless held together in some sort of mature spiritual and social background.

Roger Wilson: *Quaker Relief*, p. 109   Q

Men who have never received and have had little occasion to express the love theme or original goodness respond in a very significant manner to that first *real, spontaneous, gratuitous* kindness. Those feelings that find no expression in desperate times store themselves up in great abundance, ripen, strengthen, and strain the walls of their repository to the utmost; where the kindred spirit touches this wall it crumbles—no one responds more to kindness, no one is more sensitive to it than the desperate man.

I'm trying to say thanks.

George Jackson: *Soledad Brother*
[Prison Letters], p. 284

contamination from it, deliberately laying aside that defensive armour and allowing ourselves to get hurt too. It is painful to see and hear great distress. It may be shown as anger, which feels like an attack on us, or as grief, which makes us feel helpless and exposed. When we back away from this, the other thinks: 'I was right, my pain is intolerable—even my friend can't bear it.' Elizabeth whose husband killed himself said, 'People treated me like a leper'.

The reassuring thing is that even if we do very little, it can mean so much. If we do not know what to say, we can reach out our arms. If we are (sadly) too inhibited to touch, we can give great help by listening. If the other person cannot even talk, it is still important to be there. We often feel that these physical tokens of our care are inadequate in the face of deep human suffering; and so they are. Yet, as Jesus reminds us in his story of the Samaritan and the wounded Jew, there is something of God even in our halting offer to put the kettle on and make a cup of tea. The person who has been hurt by another loses some of the sense of human solidarity. We are reminded of our essential loneliness. A smile, a word, a touch, a hug, begins to pull down that barrier.

Every means of mending hurt has its shadow. As society's care for the sick, the mad, the deserted and the poor grew, it created structures of compassion where they could be cherished in the way I have been describing. And these structures became part of our defence against our feeling the pain of other people's hurt. It is not that hospitals, 'homes' for children and

Social workers are dealing the whole time with desperately tragic, ghastly, often hopeless human situations. One thing that has to be said in favour of them is that they are looking after the people everybody else has washed their hands of. Social work departments are often called the 'dustbin departments' for that reason. They're seeing all the nakedness of sin and violence, sexual abuse and hate and viciousness, in their everyday lives.

Nicholas Stacey, quoted in *The Listener*,
6 February 1986, p. 11

old people, or drugs to mollify depression and anxiety, are bad in themselves. But it means that we are
tempted not to feel concern or responsibility for the
suffering in our community; it can be left to the
experts and the professional carers, who can surely do
it better than we can.

But when our own commitment is withdrawn, the
love and compassion (as it seems) start to drain out of
our institutions and services. The people they serve
begin to suffer, until we may find that society's instru-
ment for mending hurts has become part of the
damaging process. Many staff, who entered their pro-
fession from a wish to cherish others, become cynical
or depressed, and no longer express compassion in
their work. Those who do not lose their ideals can find
themselves under impossible strain as they carry the
burdens of the world on their own.

Are we aware of how our own lack of love is
destroying large parts of the structures of caring
which we have set up? Do we extend our compassion
to the police, the prison staffs, the workers in mental
hospitals, and all the others who are at the frontier
where society becomes aware of the hurts which it
inflicts? And if we say Yes, it matters to us, when did
each of us last communicate it in a personal way, and
to whom? Because money, democratic support, and
letters to the press, are only substitute ways of saying
we care. Loving and cherishing happen when we
meet face to face.

I should be able to explain to you why I did that, why I didn't want to see her, but I can't. Parts of it are obvious, I guess. I was ashamed and embarrassed and so on. I was also resentful and frustrated and so on. But those are all reasons and feelings, and I wasn't reasoning or feeling anything very much at all. Things just didn't seem to matter very much. The main thing seemed to be to avoid pain . . .

I was actually much stronger than I thought, too strong. Man of steel. Pulled practically undamaged from a totally wrecked car. I could see no particular reason for going on and finishing school and going to State [University] and getting a job and living fifty more years, but that seemed to be the programme. A man of steel does what he is programmed to do.

I'm not describing this at all well. What I keep leaving out, what I don't know how to say, what I don't even want to think about, is that it was horrible. The whole time, for weeks, every morning when I woke up, every night in bed, I wanted to cry, because I couldn't stand it. Only I could stand it, and I couldn't cry. There wasn't anything to cry about.

Ursula Le Guin: *A Very Long Way From Anywhere Else*,
pp. 54–55

Working on the pain

The caring, loving response is 'first-aid', which may be enough to allow healing to happen. For we all have God-given resources for healing ourselves, in our minds as well as our bodies. There is not full agreement on how this works; but I would like to offer a model which I find helpful.

When something arouses bad feelings inside us, whether grief, anger, embarrassment, guilt or shame, we are like containers. Two things determine how effective a container is: its own strength, and the pressure of the contents. People who are genuinely able to work their way through their bad feelings to forgiveness and peace of mind can be thought of as containers strong enough to hold dangerous contents until they can make them safe. They need our care and concern; but when we think about mending hurts, we are primarily thinking of those who cannot manage this alone. We may compare some of them to containers good enough for everyday purposes, who then receive contents far more explosive than usual. Others are already almost too full of contents which are not yet made safe; so that any addition increases pressure to danger point. Some of these people suddenly explode at what seems a tiny provocation; while some of them are draining off the excess all the time in continual irritability. Others again can hold their contents, but the stress of doing so employs all their

On our farm we have a row of maple trees that illustrate the mysterious processes of adaptation. Many years ago these trees were used as fence posts for the stringing of barbed wire around the pasture. Now, fifty or sixty years later, it is possible to look at those trees and observe the way the life process shows itself in adaptation. In some places the trees fought against the barbed wire as a hostile agent, and here the trees have long and ugly scars that deface the bark and inner structure of the trees. In other places, the barbed wire has been accepted and incorporated into the life of the tree. Where this happened, the barbed wire left no mark on the tree, and all that shows is the wire entering on one side and exiting at the other ... It is natural to wonder what makes the difference in the quality of a tree's response to injury. What was there in some trees that made them injure themselves by fighting against injury? What made it possible for other trees to be able to incorporate the injuring object and become master of the barbed wire rather than its victim?

Edgar N. Jackson: *The Many Faces of Grief*, pp. 123–4

Violence is in a way like bad language—something that a person like me's been brought up with, something I got used to very early on as part of the daily scene of childhood you might say. I don't have a sort of inborn dislike of the thing like you do. As long as I can remember I've seen violence in use all round me—my mother hitting the children; my brothers and sister all whacking our mother or other children; the man downstairs bashing his wife and so on.

Tony Parker and Robert Allerton:
The Courage of his Convictions, p. 93

energies; they may be in an acute state of tension or depression. And lastly we can compare some people, those who we think of as inadequate as well as aggressive (and who cause a great deal of hurt) to containers so leaky that they cannot hold anything for long, and let it splash out indiscriminately.

This model does not explain how the bad feelings are de-toxified in our personal Sellafields, a process akin to the way we 'work through' grief. It does not recognise that different people have instinctual drives of different strengths; and it ignores the very different estimates, in different cultures, of when behaviour (and even violence) becomes hurtful. It does not look at the reasons, to be sought largely in our earliest experiences, why as containers we differ in these ways. But in spite of these omissions, I hope that it is recognisable, and helpful.

One way in which it reflects experience is that when we hold powerful and distressing feelings inside, we feel as if we might disintegrate. To whatever it is that has disturbed us is added the anxiety, at times amounting to panic, that we will fall apart. We react by retreating from a position where we can hold together love and anger at the same person, fear and hope, to a more primitive awareness, in which even our body chemistry is preparing us for the options of fight, flight, total dependency or playing dead. It feels as though these primitive reactions, with which we mastered intense anxieties when we were very small, are the only ones which might save us now.

When I am in this situation, you can help me. I have

[Priscilla Buxton on her aunt, Elizabeth Fry:]

There was no weakness or trouble of mind or body which might not safely be unveiled to her. Whatever various or opposite views, feelings or wishes might be confided to her, all came out again tinged with her own loving, hoping spirit. Bitterness of every kind died; when intrusted to her, it never reappeared. The most favourable construction possible was always put upon every transaction. No doubt her failing lay this way; but did it not give her and her example a wonderful influence? Was it not the very secret of her power with the wretched and degraded prisoners? She always could see hope for everyone; she invariably found or made some point of light. The most abandoned must have felt she did not despair for them, either for this world or another; and this it was that made her irresistible.

Mrs Francis Cresswell: *A Memoir of Elizabeth Fry*,
p. 183   Q

The potential space between baby and mother, between child and family, between individual and society or the world, depends on experience which leads to trust. It can be looked on as sacred to the individual in that it is here that the individual experiences creative living . . . the place where play can start.

By contrast, exploitation of this area leads to a pathological condition in which the individual is cluttered up with persecutory elements of which he has no way of ridding himself . . .

Psychotherapy takes place in the overlap of two areas of playing, that of the patient and that of the therapist. Psychotherapy has to do with two people playing together.

D. W. Winnicott: *Playing and Reality*, pp. 144 and 121

been describing my state as if the container had to be one mind, one body. If I feel this is so, I can perhaps exploit you by making you carry my feelings. Often enough apparently placid people, who are seething with repressed hostility, can displace anger onto all the people around, who then express it for them. Sometimes the projection of feeling has a magical power. A psychiatrist was walking round the grounds of a mental hospital with a patient, a murderer, who was mortally ill. They paused by a pit being excavated for a new building when he was seized by a panic fear that the sick man was about to throw him into the pit to kill him. He took a grip on himself, and said 'I think that you are full of the fear of death, and you can't face it, and you're putting that fear into me.' His companion immediately relaxed and said 'that's right', and then they were able to explore it together.

But you do not have to be the reluctant recipient of my feelings. There is something more positive you can do to help. The boundary which is able to contain the bad feelings, the space within which they can be de-toxified does not have to be *you* or *me*; it can be *you and me*. (I am putting this in 'I and Thou' terms, but it can also be true in a group of people.) A famous psycho-analyst says that psychotherapy, like play, does not take place inside the person, or in the outside world, but somewhere else, in a shared space between two people. Let me put this in a way more familiar to Friends. Can you believe that you can carry out of meeting for worship with you the silence which you helped to create during the meeting? And can you

The poor woman would make such a noise in roaring, and
sometimes lying along upon her belly upon the ground, with
her spirit and roaring and voice that it would set all Friends in a
heat and sweat. And I said, 'All Friends, keep to your own, lest
that which is in her get into you,' and so she affrighted the
world from our meetings . . . Another day we met about her,
and about the first hour the Life rose in Friends and said it was
done. She rose up and her countenance changed and became
white; and before it was wan and earthly; and she sat down at
my thigh as I was sitting, and lifted up her hands and said, 'Ten
thousand praise the Lord,' and did not know where she was,
and so was well.

George Fox: Journal, pp. 42–3   Q

No wonder that some who wished to give help [in the Irish
famine, 1847] gave up and fled; that others lost hope and
despaired; and others again faded with the starving into a
common grave. Old William Forster could not bear to look: 'I
have not nerve—there is no need to tell my weakness . . . it
takes too much possession of me, and almost disqualifies me
for exertion . . . I have never before passed through such suffering of mind, except when racked with unutterable intensity of
feeling in thinking of the horrors of the slave trade.' It killed
Joseph Bewley; Jacob Harvey died too, coping with the poor
emigrants to New York; and for him they wrote this magnifi-
cant epitaph: 'by all who knew him he was loved as few are
loved, and he has died and left not an enemy on the earth.'

John Ormerod Greenwood: Friends and Relief,
pp. 34–35   Q

then imagine that, meeting someone who has been wounded, you invite her or him into that silence? Because we believe that, in that silence, there is two-way communication with God and with each other; we believe that needs are known there and answered; we believe that no load is too heavy in that place because it is God who carries it there.

How does this work—in practice, and with someone who doesn't share your Quaker or Christian suppositions, but needs your help? Sometimes that peace which you carry—which is carrying you—may reach to me, and I know that the internal pressure is less, and anxiety can abate. But often it is not like this; and when I feel that we have established a space between us which can contain the bad material, I release it into that space. Then you feel your own containing strength being tested as you are surrounded and penetrated by my hate, my anger, my despair, my grief. Your own old scars begin to ache. You are tempted to say 'Don't throw all your rubbish at me! I'm not responsible!' If you do so, this confirms my feeling that what I am carrying is unbearable—you can no more face it than I can, and I may as well give up. I would prefer you to gather up all my pain and take it away with you, no matter what you then do with it. But in the long run this will not help either. I will never learn from my experience, or be able to master it, if I just use you as my psychological refuse-collector. Moreover, although you accepted my burdens willingly, if you take them on yourself endlessly, they are almost certain to damage you. This may sound

27

Macbeth: Canst thou not minister to a mind diseased,
Pluck from the memory a rooted sorrow,
Raze out the written troubles of the brain,
And with some sweet oblivious antidote
Cleanse the stuff'd bosom of that perilous
stuff
Which weighs upon the heart?

Doctor: Therein the patient
Must minister to himself.

William Shakespeare: *Macbeth*, Act V scene 3

Everyone is potentially a tool of healing for anyone else. And it often happens that healing power works outside the Church and the ministry. The fact that Jesus gave the disciples responsibility for healing and casting out demons does not constitute a special prerogative on the part of the minister. Every Christian receives this charge, and each of us should take it seriously in our relation to one another.

Paul Tillich: *The Boundaries of our Being*, p. 50

fanciful, but it is familiar enough to nurses and social workers, who call it 'burn-out'.

I need you to take this great lump of pain which I feel inside me. I want you to look at it, and feel it, and think about it. Perhaps you can blunt some of its edges, soften it a little with your tears, or throw it up in the air and catch it, to show me it is not so heavy as I thought. Perhaps you can take a measure and show me its proper size. Perhaps you could hold it just for a little, while I get on my feet again. But then you should give it back to me, because it is my load and my task. You may carry away a little of the poison, but the real task of making it safe can only be done by me. I may want you to be stern with me, to strip my self-pity off the bundle. But you have shown me that one can think about it, weigh it, lift it, change it. And I know that this has been costly to you: thank you for taking my load for me for a short while.

Does it sound as if this is a job needing great expertise, and great personal strength? I hope not, because each of us is being asked to do it all the time, whenever someone shares a little of their pain with me or you. But we don't always do it very well. The hurt each of us carries gets in the way, and we 'switch off', or 'push' our own advice defensively. Or we over-identify with them, cutting ourselves off from that inner peace and balance which the Holy Spirit gives us for our lifeline as we go forward to reach them in the turbulent waters. We can all learn to do better; but it is not true that we need enormous strength. Indeed, if we were invulnerable we could not do it at all, because

Some of you may say, 'I shall go into the city slums, into the war-stricken areas, into work with share-croppers and dis-possessed miners. And in the world's sufferings I shall find God.' And I would reply, Yes, many have found Him in these settings and scenes of squalor and tragedy. But He whom you seek *is already there in the midst of the suffering*, bearing its load, before you ever became a bearer of the world's suffering. It is because He was already speaking within you that you went to share the burden.

Thomas Kelly: *The Eternal Promise*, pp. 104–5   Q

the other person's suffering could not penetrate our defences. In my work I have had many interviews with people in distress. Sometimes through my professional skills I could be helpful; but I know that the meetings which achieved most were those where I felt so inadequate and confused that I could not trust myself at all. That is when we listen most intently in our helplessness, searching for pointers in what we are being told and in the whisper of the Holy Spirit in our hearts.

I am finding it easier to talk about this process in metaphor than in a straight description, so let me give you two examples. I remember a sixteen-year-old boy for whom I was responsible, who cut his wrists while his adoptive parents were on a trip overseas. When they were back this father hurried to see him. 'Why did you do it?' The boy tried to explain that he felt that he had let his parents down by his poor exam results. 'But that's not true, we were very proud of your results, you did much better than we expected.' The boy tried again, saying how he felt that nobody liked him because he wasn't worth liking. Again his father told him that wasn't so, look how many friends he had, and so on. The boy was asking his father to share and help contain his feelings of worthlessness; and the father was finding those feelings so painful to contemplate that he could only tell his son that it wasn't so, he wasn't *really* feeling like that. This insincere reassurance is the imitation, the perversion, of what I am trying to describe.

In contrast, there was a time when we had a young

The wounded surgeon plies the steel
That questions the distempered part;
Beneath the bleeding hands we feel
The sharp compassion of the healer's art
Resolving the enigma of the fever chart.

T. S. Eliot: *East Coker*, IV

man from Northern Ireland living with us, who
wanted to break his previous links with the IRA. For
his first fortnight he was shy and on his best
behaviour. Then one night he came in drunk, and
crashed to his room threatening anyone who came
near him. My wife and I went and sat quietly by him,
ignoring shouts of 'Fuck off!' After a bit he started to
cry, and amid his tears he talked about his childhood
and recent life. What with the drink, and the tears,
and his accent, we could understand very little of
what he was saying; but like a refrain he kept saying,
'At least I never killed anybody!' We hardly said a
word—but something in us, unjudging, accepting,
peaceful, silently spoke to him. After a long period he
became calm, and went to sleep. Next day, he was a bit
embarrassed at first, but the whole relationship was
richer and deeper. Though we never knew most of
what he tried to tell us, we had shared the guilt and
hurt.

I believe we can all do this work, in God's strength,
not our own. I also believe that we all meet occasions
in which we are being told to do it, in the same way as
we are sometimes told to speak in a Friends' meeting.
It then becomes a matter of holy obedience to
obey—to find our courage, to meet the other person in
her or his anger, depression, disorientation or frozen
state, to listen, to let the Holy Spirit speak through us,
to trust in that strength, wisdom and goodness which
(we claim) underpins our world. This will usually be a
face-to-face encounter, and we must not look for
excuses to avoid this. But we must remember too that

Deborah was not convinced. 'Maybe you doubt that I saw it at all.'

'That is the one thing that I do not doubt,' the doctor said. 'But you see, I have no part in what is to be done on the wards; I am not an administrative doctor.'

Deborah saw the match lighting dry fuel. 'What good is your reality, when justice fails and dishonesty is glossed over and the ones who keep faith suffer? What good is your reality then?'

'Look here,' Furii said. 'I never promised you a rose-garden. I never promised you perfect justice . . . and I never promised you peace or happiness. My help is so that you can be free to fight for all these things. The only reality I offer is challenge, and being well is being free to accept it or not at whatever level you are capable. I never promise lies, and the rose-garden world of perfection is a lie—and a bore too!'

Hannah Green: *I Never Promised You a Rose-Garden*, p. 101

God can use us to mend hurts in other ways. A friend of ours was in the act of looking round for the means to kill herself, when she suddenly knew that a Friend from her previous Meeting was loving her and praying for her. She stopped, sat on her bed, and felt healing flow into her. From that moment the whole shape of her life began to change.

Those who cannot manage and digest their own feelings of hurt need our help to work through them, whether this comes in a chance encounter, in a friendship, with a professional therapist, or through the spiritual ministry of healing, of which we still understand so little. But it is not the end of the matter. The wrong still exists, and so does the person who has caused it. Just to see him or her may be enough to reawaken the same feelings, as intense as when they were fresh. If we are looking for proper healing, forgiveness, harmony and justice, there is often much more to be done: reconciliation, making amends, making a new start and planning how things can be different in the future.

Reconciliation is, of course, the ultimate aim of peace making. It is a word of power and beauty which implies, etymologically, the re-establishment of a council; as though there had once been a council of humankind that had been fractured by our errors and ill-doings. Many feel that all the impediments to peace can be removed by reconciliation. Others think, however, that the correction of injustices is sufficient.

Adam Curle: *True Justice*, p. 43   Q

... that private differences which may happen among any Friends or brethren, be ended by some Friend in the wisdom and counsel of God, with as much privacy as may be—without troubling or disturbing the public meetings or churches with them, and without public reflections upon persons ... In the restoring and healing spirit of Christ both the offended and the offender may for the Truth's sake submit to the power of God in his people ... with such Friends as they with the parties concerned shall call to their assistance.

Epistle from Friends met in London,
the 26th of Third Month, 1673   Q

The aim of our new court will not be to punish, not to create suffering but to diminish it, not to give the offender what he 'deserves' (which of us is qualified to determine that?) but to identify and meet both his and the victim's needs in relation to society; not to try to deter by punishment but by more constructive means; and one of the singular differences between our present practice and the new one is that we shall expect and very often receive the co-operation of the offender.

Six Quakers look at Crime and Punishment, p. 17   Q

Reconciliation

Adam Curle calls reconciliation 'a word of power and beauty' and he says it is the ultimate goal of peace-making. But one can also use the word in a more restricted way, of a process where people or groups caught up in a cycle of wrong and counter-wrong can try to find a way out, sharing their needs and feelings and entering into one another's viewpoints. This is the way that I shall be using it. Mennonites and Quakers in the USA have been developing different forms of mediation process between individuals, and there is a growing awareness that disputes and griev-ances traditionally dealt with by the courts can be more constructively settled by mediation. This is because the style of court proceedings creates a win-ner and a loser; when the loser is compelled to mend the hurt, a new sense of grievance is created. But in a process of reconciliation, both parties can recognise the pain of one other and agree to resolve it.

When I worked with boys with emotional prob-lems, we had a youngster whose father had aban-doned the family and was now a successful artist in another country. One evening, Owen, a young teacher, arrived at my house breathless with anger. He had been playing a game where several of the boys had been hiding in the corridors and jumping on him as he passed. Suddenly he looked at his watch and told them he had to go to supervise a homework group. As he went off, this boy ran after him and leapt

And so we went to our inn again, and there were two desperate fellows fighting so that none durst come nigh to part them, but I was moved in the Lord's power to go to them, and when I had loosed their hands, I held one of them by one hand and the other by the other hand; and I showed them the evil of their doings, and convinced them, and reconciled them to each other that they were loving and very thankful, so that people admired at it.

George Fox: *Journal*, p. 229   Q

on his back, hurting him. In order not to show his anger, he swung the boy on to the floor and went off without a word. Shortly afterwards he heard that the boy had been throwing bricks at his motorbike and had smashed the headlamp glass. Before I could go and fetch the boy, he arrived, also extremely angry and demanding I should 'do something about Owen'. I asked him to say why he was angry. I had to ask Owen several times not to interrupt him. The boy described the incident much as the teacher had; when he told us how he had been dumped on the floor, he said, 'And then he went off without even looking back to see if I was hurt'. He kept repeating this. As he clearly wasn't really hurt, I took a risk and said 'Just like your father did.' He went on talking without a pause, but both of us realised that the subject had changed, and he was now describing how he felt about his father; how he had gone off without caring, how he would not support the family now that he was well off though they were still in poverty. When he knew that we had heard him out, he could listen to Owen's story, how the horseplay had hurt his back, and how he had tried to avoid losing his temper. The boy spontaneously offered to do odd jobs at the weekend to pay for the headlight; and I interposed again to say to Owen, who was gifted in art, that I would like him to paint a picture for the boy to hang over his bed. A more skilful mediator would have brought it to a point where Owen suggested this spontaneously; for when the boy went, Owen told me rather crossly that he didn't see why he should do something for a boy

What now of the reconciler? 'Blessed are the peacemakers; for they shall be called the children of God.' His heart is torn by the thought of man's estrangement from man, no less than the prophet's is by man's estrangement from God. He feels laid upon him the ministry of reconciliation between individuals and between groups. But he sees divisions and enmities as infinitely complex situations to which there is no single or simple solution. He accepts the apparent limitations of the minds of those who are divided, and tries to work within these limitations. He tries to reassure and to suggest actions which will provide reassurance; he tries to wean gently from pathological attitudes. To act therapeutically in this way, to exercise this almost pastoral vocation, he must not impose his own solutions, he must not always have his own axe to grind. He must be acceptable.

'For the sake of being acceptable,' argues the prophet, 'You water down the Gospel. You soft-pedal the truth. You are afraid that if you let them know what you really think, they will laugh at you and you will lose what influence you may have. In the end—if it hasn't happened already—you will become corrupted and lose your faith and it will be left to others to carry it on. Moreover, every time you suggest a compromise you betray your principles.'

W. Grigor McClelland: *The Prophet and the Reconciler*, p. 4   Q

who had first hurt him and then damaged his property. But I was able to convince him that there was a potential for future healing in the fact that the boy had identified him with his father—but only if Owen could show that, unlike the father, he was prepared to look back, and care, and make amends when he (even unintentionally) caused pain.

In the Mennonite model of mediation, each party is asked to agree to a face-to-face meeting. After the mediators have introduced themselves, the contenders each tell their story without interruption from the other; this usually creates an agenda for a discussion which tries to deal both with practical issues and underlying feelings. They are tempted to defend their positions. But the mediators encourage them to look instead at where their interests lie (which are not necessarily opposed) and to start work on the least confused problem on the agenda. They help one another to understand what they have felt; they look at ways in which both parties' needs can be met. The final agreement should be balanced and workable, saying who should do what and when, and what should happen if problems recur. It may well include opportunities for increasing contacts between the parties, to build up understanding and friendship.

This mutual understanding is an essential part of this process. As the saying goes, to understand everything is to forgive everything. This is because guilt, as well as pain, walls us in. Rather than accept our own responsibility for what we do, we blame the other—and we can usually find some pretext for being angry.

* The story is told in *John, 21:15ff*

The wise ruler says:
I take no action and the people are transformed of themselves;
I prefer stillness and the people are rectified of themselves;
I do not interfere and the people prosper of themselves;
I am free from desire and the people of themselves become
    simple like the uncarved block.
Lao Tzu: Tao te Ching, LXXIII.179

We often noticed that we had an argument every time that I
had reconciled another couple. The couple had invested their
violence in me, and I was investing it in my wife. I have always
been aware my workshop provided a place where I could
discharge my violence. Working on wood, steel or gold, with
hammer, saw or file, I could invest the violence which my
patients had poured out on me in the consulting room.
Paul Tournier: The Violence Inside, p. 71

Mediation sessions are often stormy; sometimes the anger has to be brought into the space between us and them before it can be seen for what it is, understood, accepted, and exchanged for the bad feelings of the other. Both Owen and the boy had some right to be angry; yet they were unable to hold on to their own anger when they grasped what each other was feeling. 'Simon bar Jonah, do you love me?' asked Jesus. Was he crying as he said it? Did the pain of his previous rejection show in his face?*

The role of the mediator has a special quality. People are often drawn into it because they have a passionate desire to bring harmony and a belief that they can see the issues more clearly than those involved. This may be true; but at the beginning they are not carrying the feelings which count for so much in the situation. During the mediation process they may find that those feelings, by some mysterious means, are now inside them. But now they have lost their objectivity and are as confused as the protagonists. There is a paradox here, familiar to family therapists, marriage guidance councillors, industrial conciliators and others: how to provide the *milieu* in which facts and feelings can be really experienced without being drawn into the turmoil. The reconciler must believe that there is a solution. But to be valid it must be discovered by the parties involved, in a joint search; if it comes from him or her, it will either be rejected out of hand or adopted and then subtly sabotaged. This demands great forbearance: not only in not making suggestions, but also in containing the

The assumption that peacemaking in the international field is solely a matter of disinterested personal service has never been built on sound foundations. A reconciler will hardly appear to the eyes of statesmen as a detached arbiter or mediator to whom they may wish to open their hearts about the mutual entanglements . . . Maybe he is able, under the guidance of the spirit, to impress them with a quality different from what they normally expect from a politician. This, of course, is his great chance and his hope. All the same, he will be placed by them on the chessboard of politics as a pawn to be used, or as a useful go-between through whom the opponent may be informed, misled, or influenced in some other way.

Richard K. Ullmann: *The Dilemmas of a Reconciler*,
p. 4   Q

The effectiveness of the Quaker interpreters [in the Nigerian Civil War 1967–70] in changing perceptions of the parties in conflict is impossible to measure, but some things can be said. The Quaker influence was one of several supporting a policy in Lagos aimed towards negotiating peace. Although such a settlement was not achieved, the military victory was followed by a magnaminity towards the defeated rebels hardly paralleled in recent history . . . One qualified observer said he thought the remarkably peaceful end to hostilities was in part due to the way in which the Quakers had constantly tried to straighten out perceptions distorted by fear and anger.

Mike Yarrow: *Quaker Experiences in International Conciliation*, p. 252–3   Q

painful feelings experienced during the process, not passing this pain back to the quarrelling parties, but finding one's own way of resolving it without further hurt to anyone.

The model for reconciliation is the person-to-person encounter, in the presence of someone else, who doesn't impose decisions but enables a healing process to take place. Mediation between large groups can follow this pattern, but only when those present are truly representative. They must be close enough to the hurt of their people to voice it convincingly, and—after mediation—to persuade them that it has been heard and recognised. In Northern Ireland, well-meaning peacemakers persuaded some community leaders to enter into reconciliatory moves, but the whole process moved too fast, and the leaders were later killed by their own people as traitors. The experience reminds us how essential it is that group mediation does not take place only between leaders, but is mirrored by humbler encounters. If trust is not fostered at every level, renewed problems can rapidly destroy the agreement that has been reached. But I have found that even people in extreme positions passionately want to be heard and understood, and not only for propaganda purposes. The moderates who say 'Deny them a platform' are usually not frightened of the lies and exaggerations but of having to recognise the elements of hurt and justice in the extremist's position; in such a situation it is the moderate, not the extremist, who is working against reconciliation.

* The story is told in *I Samuel, 24*

Too long have Christians in this country [South Africa] attempted to avoid genuine reconciliations by proclaiming a 'unification' that rests on a cloaking of guilt and a pious silence about evil ... Reconciliation is not merely 'feeling good' but *doing what is right*. Besides, reconciliation does not occur between 'whites' and 'non-whites', or between ruler and ruled. Genuine reconciliation does not occur between oppressor and oppressed, it occurs between persons, persons who face each other in their authentic, vulnerable, and yet hopeful humanity. And therefore liberation ... is inevitably bound up with reconciliation. And forgiveness.

Allan Boesak: *The Finger of God*, p. 68

An independent person is not always needed as mediator. Both the disputants have the power within them to forgive and make amends. Often, if one of them can escape from the cycle of hurt, he or she will be able to use this power and put the other in touch with it. You will remember, when David was 'on the run' from King Saul, how he hid one day in a cave. Saul came into the cave and crouched down to relieve himself. David's men hoped their leader would kill his persecutor; but David just cut a piece of Saul's cloak; and when the King had left the cave he followed him out and called to him. Saul was astonished that David had not killed him. But David spoke his griev-ances and said, 'One wrong begets another, as the old saying goes, yet I will never lift my hand against you.' 'Is that you, David, my son?' said Saul, 'The right is on your side, not mine; you have treated me so well, I have treated you so badly.' And the two men came to understand one another and made peace.*

The art of reconciliation, like that of cherishing, has its perverted image, which looks like it but has no healing power. This comes when agreement is forced, against the wishes of the heart—under the pressure of power, or logic, or status, or public opinion; when there is intimidation, or the inducements of short-term advantage. It happens at every level, from the little child compelled to say an insincere 'sorry' to the trade-union delegation out-manoeuvred by the dip-lomatic skills of the management team; from the ado-lescent agreeing to a probation order to the governments making agreements at the behest of

* These sayings are reported in *Luke 12:13* and *Matthew 5:23–24*

A Satyagrahi must never forget the distinction between evil and the evil-doer. He must not harbour ill-will or bitterness against the latter. He may not even employ needlessly offensive language against the evil person, however unrelieved his evil might be. For it should be an article of faith with every Satyagrahi that there is none so fallen in this world but can be converted by love.

Mohandas Gandhi: article in *Young India*, 8 August 1929

Henry Kissinger. This perversion of reconciliation may bring a momentary calm; but unless it is then followed by genuine, effective peacemaking, the residue of bitterness does its deadly work in secret until pain has turned to anger strong enough to break out again. Jesus would not be made a mediator for forced reconciliation: 'Who made me a judge over you?' But he spoke of true reconciliation as an essential precondition for religious worship.*

I have suggested that reconciliation in its basic form occurs between two people face-to-face. But something like it can occur when one of the parties will not or cannot take part in the process. I know a physically handicapped young man who is serving a prison sentence (thirteen years so far) for a crime committed by someone else. His cheerfulness and goodness, which are widely recognised, come from a decision which he made at the start, that he would not be bitter; and he has kept to this even though there has been no answering attempt at reconciliation from those who put him in prison—neither the paramilitaries who committed the crime, nor the police who extracted a false and forced confession. There can be a sudden awareness of the necessity of forgiveness which may change me, whether I am the victim or the assailant. Even if a person whom we have hurt or disappointed is dead, we may still find where we can confess and be absolved, whether in church, in group therapy, or in simple friendship.

Once, in a psychodrama, I cast someone in the role of my father, and we acted out a time when I felt my

My conclusion is that though my enemy and I cannot always, in the absence of justice, reach a point of agreement which makes conflict unnecessary, there *is* a perspective from which 'all our righteousness is as filthy rags', our differences—however precious to us—insignificant, and the question of who wins quite irrelevant. It is this realisation which should drive us, even in the heat of conflict, to seek God's forgiveness. My enemy and I have many differences, some of which have brought us to the point of conflict; the one thing we share is the need to be forgiven.

Kenneth Kaunda: *Kaunda on Violence*, p. 184

father had abandoned me, far too young, to the unfeeling atmosphere of a boarding school. During this we exchanged roles, and I found myself experiencing something of his guilt and pain at the decision. After this the therapist asked me how my relationship with him had developed during adolescence. I said that we liked and respected each other, but had neither argued and fought, nor been really close. The therapist told me to face my 'father' and grip his arms and try to force him backwards. He pushed back and we struggled fiercely with each other for several minutes. Then we were encouraged to come together in a tight embrace. We struggled again, hugged again, struggled and hugged. The therapist asked me if I needed to push once more; but now I said No, something had really changed for me, and there had been a reconciliation with the dead. Several of the group were crying—not only for us, but for the feelings which resonated in them as they shared the experience.

It is widely recognised that we see in our enemies the qualities which we deny in ourselves: *they* are to blame, *they* are the greedy ones, the unreasonable, the hostile. To be reconciled to them is to embrace what we would prefer to disown; it is hard. But when we have done it, we are more whole, and therefore we feel enriched. My wife Diana and I will never forget when a fellow-Quaker at last came and told us that he secretly disliked us, and why. Old disagreements in business meetings and elsewhere were re-examined together, and we each explained how we had felt and

It is a mistake to consider the objects of punishment as being deterrent or reformative or preventive and nothing else . . . the ultimate justification of any punishment is not that it is deterrent, but that it is the emphatic denunciation by the community of a crime.

Lord Denning: *Evidence to the Royal Commission on Capital Punishment 1953.*

why we said certain things. The joy and liberation which followed for each of us was intense, and we all still feel enriched by it.

But we must be clear that reconciliation, in this sense of meeting, comprehending, and working to prevent the future following the pattern of the past, is not always possible. The demand for justice, the desire for revenge, may prevent it. Quakers in particular seem to have a horror of revenge as a motive. We need to remember that, in the interests of social harmony, law-abiding citizens have voluntarily surrendered their rights of retaliation to the state. It may be true that when the state takes revenge, nothing constructive has been achieved. But it is also true that if not even this is done, the hurt remains with the person who has been wronged. Where the burden of suffering is clearly on one side, the burden of wrong-doing on the other, it is a kind of insult to tell the victim that she or he should be reconciled. We are told that there is no peace without justice. How are we to meet the claims of justice without forging the next link in the chain of hurt?

As persons setting Negroes free in our province are bound by law to maintain them in case they have need of relief, some in the time of my youth who scrupled to keep slaves for term of life were wont to detain their young Negroes in their service without wages till they were thirty years of age. With this custom I so far agreed that I, as companion to another Friend in excuting the will of a deceased Friend, once sold a Negro lad till he might attain the age of thirty years, and applied the money to the use of the estate.

With abasement of heart I may now say that sometimes as I have sat in a meeting with my heart exercised towards that awful being who respecteth not persons nor colours, and looked on this Negro lad, I've felt that all was not clear in my mind respecting him: and as I have attended to this exercise and fervently sought the Lord, it hath appeared to me that I should make some restitution; but in what way I saw not till lately ... and my mind for a time was covered with darkness and sorrow. Under this sore affliction my mind was softened to receive instruction, and I now first perceived that as I had been one of the two executors who had sold this Negro lad nine years longer than is common for our own [white] children to serve, so I should now offer part of my substance to redeem the last half of the nine years.

John Woolman: *Journal*, entry for 11th. 6mo. 1769   Q

My dearly beloved Sister,

      ... I have been with James Naylor in the prison three times since I came to this city, and true love and life are springing up in him; he is made willing to lie under all, and would do anything that might in the wisdom of God be seen convenient for taking off all occasion [of reproach to Friends because of his actions], as much as in him lies, either by public recantation (which I do not judge serviceable for exalting the Truth) or in any other way ...

Alexander Parker: *Letter to Margaret Fell* London,
15th of 4th mo. 1658   Q

Restitution

Two years ago we were at Corrymeela Reconciliation Centre in Northern Ireland with ten families from the two sides of the community in Londonderry. Several of the teenagers went off with one of the leaders to camp on Rathlin Island, and it emerged at the end of the week that two of them (a protestant and a catholic!) had robbed a collection box in a church there. We talked to the two boys, and they agreed to come back to Corrymeela for a day, where they worked really hard scrubbing, cleaning and polishing an area which the staff had been too busy to do. They were paid for this; and before they left, the staff told them that they had now completely made up for the disappointment they had caused and would be welcome back at any time. From Corrymeela they went with their earnings to the rector of the church, who was extremely surprised and grateful. He told them the church had been robbed several times before, but never had anyone come back to put things right. Finally, when we took them home, we had to tell their parents what they had done; but we were able to say at the same time how hard they had worked to restore what had been stolen, not only the money but the trust and the good reputation of Corrymeela in its neighbourhood.

This way of handling wrongs accepts the reality of what has happened and the right of the sufferer to 'have something done about it'. It accepts that the

I am moved to write to you to take heed of putting men to death for stealing cattle or money, &c: for the thieves in the old time were to make restitution ... Mind the laws of God in the Scriptures and the Spirit that gave them forth and let that be your rule in executing judgement; and show mercy, that you receive mercy from God, the judge of all.

George Fox: 'Letter to Derby magistrates from prison, 1651.' (*Journal*, p. 66)   Q

The early [childhood] wish to make reparation is added to the capacity for love. Constructive activities gain more impetus because the child unconsciously feels that in this way he is restoring loved people whom he has damaged. This impetus never loses its strength, though very often it is not recognised in ordinary life. The irrevocable fact that none of us is ever entirely free from guilt has very valuable aspects because it implies the never fully exhausted wish to make reparation and to create in whatever way we can. All forms of social service benefit by this urge.

Melanie Klein: *Our Adult World and Its Roots in Infancy*, p. 16

perpetrator is in most cases feeling guilty, or at least humiliated to have been detected. But it offers him or her an opportunity to regain the good opinion of the sufferer and the community, and to be seen as a person who can give as well as take away, who can right wrongs as well as cause them.

Restitution as a means of mending hurts has been criticised. It is said that it does not meet the demands of justice: it offers an easy way out, because the restitution does not measure up to the harm done to the victim; the offender at the end is no worse off than if she or he had never done wrong, and so is tempted to offend again; and our natural sense of justice demands that the offender should suffer in turn.

To take the last of these objections first, it is not at all obvious that retaliation—pain for pain—is essential to our feeling of justice. There are reasons to think that the desire to make reparation lies very deep in the human psyche, and appears at a very early stage of life. A deep sense of our power to do harm is what underpins belief in 'original sin'; it is the root of many of our most valuable activities and actions. In friendship, love and family life, we acknowledge the value of the spontaneous wish to make amends, even in small or symbolic ways: the bunch of flowers which says 'sorry', or the unexpected service given us by someone who wants to show that he or she is 'not all bad'. We set such importance on this kind of restitution and its symbols that we insist that our children apologise even when we know they don't mean it!

By contrast, the desire to inflict pain for pain has

Like nearly all women in my situation, I had a vision one night that phantom protectors had come to avenge me . . . But immediately, almost in the same second, I brushed it aside, deciding I did not want my own fascists. Better that all these monsters die off in their country villas, enjoying their retirement on pensions worthy of executioners. I would not want any band of killers to take vengence on them for me. The last thing I wish is to resemble them . . . I fear that what I am saying may qualify as 'non-resistance to evil' [Tolstoy], and if so I must accept that I am a 'non-resister'—though I wish there were some other name for it.

Nadeshda Mandelstam: *Hope Abandoned*, p. 689

* Examples of Jesus' anger may be found in *Luke, 11*

I do believe—and I can't prove it—that there is a certain amount of violence in the world, and if violence is met by violence then there is double the amount of violence in the world. And this is what's happening all over the world. But if you meet violence by doing nothing then there's not more violence in the world but the same amount. And if you accept the violence on yourself and answer violence by non-violence, answer hatred by love, then by that much the amount of violence in the world is lessened. I am quite convinced in my mind that if people were to do this consistently, we could eliminate violence within a generation.

Will Warren: Talk to International Fellowship of Reconciliation, 1977   Q

very doubtful claims to justice, because it ignores most of the interests of the victim—as well as the offender. We know that it too has deep psychological roots, in the magical belief that we can rid ourselves of pain by causing someone else to feel it. When as a teacher I came upon a youngster being cruel to another one, I felt a surge of feelings—and with them came the urge to pay him in his own coin. Often enough I did this, verbally if not physically. But I know that, to a large extent, this was a selfish impulse. I was looking for relief for myself. It did not mend the hurt he caused the other child; it did not even help to prevent him doing so again.

I am not talking here about the aggressive and assertive drive which is part of our biological endowment, but about the range of conscious feeling from irritation to fury. I recognise that there is such a thing as generous and altruistic anger. Jesus was a very angry man,* but it would be hard to prove him selfish. For most of us, if we see a fellow creature being abused, selfish and unselfish elements are mixed in our anger. What I an concerned with here is what we do with our feelings. If we are in control of them, we can use them to change structures and so, indirectly, contribute to the work of healing, or at least prevention. Even our rage at people may spring so obviously from our love for them that it plays a constructive part in our wish to help them. But all too often, whatever our motives, the result of our anger is that other people are left with hurt or angry feelings of their own.

Our personal feelings about retribution have been

I speak not against any magistrate's or people's defending themselves against foreign invasions, or making use of the sword to suppress the violent or evildoers within their borders (for this the present state of things may and doth require . . .). But yet there is a better state, which the Lord hath already brought some into, and which nations are to expect and travel towards.

Isaac Penington: *Works* [2nd Edition, vol I, p. 448] Q

The postulations which we are advancing involve a reversal of many familiar values . . . Highly valued is the idea of human justice, reflecting the justice of a just God. The value of the undiscoverable, the unknowable, has a more elusive appeal, and the ability to relinquish the notion of retributive justice is not fully within human capacity, even though tentative efforts continue to be made to explore these dimensions of uncertainty.

Jack Kahn: *Job's Illness*, p. 134

reinforced by our education. As children, when we
felt bad and worthless and were appalled at what we
had just done, most of us were not helped to put
things right with the other person and recover our
self-respect; instead we were taught that if we ourselves were deprived, even degraded, the matter
would be over—though neither forgiven nor forgot-
ten. Thus we were educated into believing that
humiliation and suffering are an essential part of
justice. But it goes still further. Because our wayward
impulses were controlled in this way, many of us
unconsciously feel that badness is only kept in check
by harshness, not by understanding and love. The
calls in society for executions, floggings, and
imprisonment for life stem from this illusion that it is
only violent controls which prevent chaos from breaking out all round us—and not only round us but
inside us too. In the country district where I used to
live, social controls were generally effective; but the
fear of them breaking down led to frequent calls for
judicial harshness and a wish to see the death penalty
restored. I now live in a city where controls seem to
have broken down. Many of my friends have known
the violent death of someone close to them. Yet from
this harsh experience almost all of them would say
that to respond with force, whether personal or
official, will only perpetuate our situation. They do
not want revenge.

Similarly, when I was working with deviant and
deprived children, and almost all disciplinary matters
were decided by the whole community on a basis of

[Reasons why punishment should be avoided in a hostel for delinquent children:]

The fundamental reason is that I consider punishment contrary to Christian teaching, whatever its expediency; but as even Christians do not agree on this point, I shall concern myself for the moment with empirical, rather than religious or moral reasons . . .

1. It establishes a base motive for conduct [i.e. fear].
2. It has been tried and has failed; or alternatively, it has been so misused in the past as to destroy its usefulness now.
3. It militates against the establishment of the relationship which we consider necessary between staff and children—a relationship in which the child must feel himself to be loved.
4. Many delinquent children, and adults, are seeking punishment as a means of assuaging their guilt-feelings [over matters quite different from the present offence].
5. When the offender has 'paid for' his crime, he can 'buy' another with an easy conscience.

W. David Wills: *The Barns Experiment*,
pp. 17 and 22   Q

* These stories are told in *John 8:1–11* and *Luke 19:1–10*

putting things right, I was able to see how the victims feel supported and protected by this approach. It was moving to see how much they wanted to accept the evidence of contrition, how much they wanted to forgive. Provided we could ensure that it worked effectively, those who had been hurt were satisfied; it was outsiders, not directly involved, who became angry and told me that this was a sentimental option which did not face the realities of injustice. They were afraid of pain, hurt, violence and the breakdown of order; and their fear made them violent. Those who had already experienced this breakdown recognised that restitution offered them a way out.

You will recall that Jesus rejected the law of retribution when they dragged a woman from her lover's arms into his presence; and that he said 'Today salvation has come to this house' when Zacchaeus offered reparation for the money he had extorted from the poor.*

Sometimes it may be hard to see how one could ever make restitution for certain things, either because of the nature of the deed or because the person injured is absent. But, as with reconciliation, the principle can be extended beyond the face-to-face encounter. I know a young man who was thought, at the age of three, to have caused the death of his baby sister. As far as I know, he has never said whether he accepts the guilt for this or not; indeed for many years he refused to speak at all, and was classified as a severely damaged child. Today he is well-adjusted and happily married and it is surely no accident that he chose to

[William Edmondson complained to the Privy Council in Dublin of how his parish priest persecuted Friends.] The privy council resented it, being contrary to all law and rule; so sent an order to the priest and apparitor to appear before the Council. They came and were sharply reproved, and had been punished, for the Chancellor said he would make them examples; but that I told him we desired nothing but to be quiet and live peaceably in our callings and that they would desist from their cruelty . . . So I forgave them and let all fall.

William Edmondson: *Journal*, p. 43   Q

* Michel Goldberg's story is told in his autobiography *Namesake*, pp. 73–87

In the Old Testament, personal rights are protected by a divinely established system of retribution. Every evil must be requited. The aim of retribution is to establish a proper community . . . That is the purpose of the law. Jesus takes up this declaration of the divine will and affirms the power of retribution to convict and overcome evil, and to ensure the fellowship of the disciples as the true Israel. By exercising the right type of retribution evil is to be overcome and thus the true disciple will prove himself. The right way to requite evil, according to Jesus, is not to resist it.

Dietrich Bonhoeffer: *The Cost of Discipleship*, pp. 126–7

work as an ambulance driver.

Is there a payment for the damage caused by a rape, or the murder of a child? The short answer must be No. But this line of reasoning also applies to retribution. Do you remember the trial of Adolf Eichmann in Israel, and the absurdity of weighing his judicial execution against the horrors of his share of the holocaust? Michel Goldberg, a French Jew, went to Bolivia to kill Klaus Barbie, the so-called 'butcher of Lyons', who was responsible during the war for the death of his father and more than 10,000 other people. Then, as he held his gun and looked at Barbie three metres away, he knew it would be meaningless to murder him. 'I did kill a Nazi in La Paz,' he wrote, 'but not the one I had planned to kill . . . I killed myself, the person I had been up to then.'*

Justice eludes us. Like beauty, it is something which we can believe in, recognise, reason about, learn to understand better—even though all earthly examples of it have their imperfection. I believe that the process of restitution must start with the victim and assailant agreeing: either the victim asks, or the assailant offers, and they discuss it in the presence of a mediator or a representative group until there is an agreement which *feels* right (though it can not be proved to be just) to all concerned. If this is done, restitution comes closer to what I have learnt about true justice than the infliction of pain ever can; because justice, surely, is concerned with the restoration of harmony, the removal of hurts and occasions of wrong.

The basis of the system [for treating the insane in 1797] generally adopted, was the position *that fear is the great principle by which the insane are to be governed*; and the practical consequences deduced from it were that their attendants should commence their intercourse with them by an appearance of austerity, and perhaps the display of physical prowess; in fact, that in some cases of violent excitement the cudgel and the whip were the most suitable instruments of coercion.

We believe it may be said that the Retreat commenced with an assent to the general correctness of these views; and though they could not fail to be modified by the good sense and feeling of the committee of management, it must be admitted that they were acted upon to an extent which, with our present knowledge, we can hardly contemplate without surprise.

The investigating mind of George Jepson had often, previously to his appointment of Superintendant, led him to query the beneficial results resulting from this system of management ... On an occasion soon after his introduction into office, after the exercise of some severity towards a violent patient, he passed a sleepless night in anxious cogitations. He felt satisfied that his mode of treatment in this case had tended to irritate rather than control the patient's diseased feelings; and he determined to try the effect of an opposite system ... Following steadily, but cautiously, the guidance of his judgement and feelings, his observations and experience soon led him to abandon the system of terror, and to adopt that which presumed the patient to be generally capable of influence through the kindly affections of the heart; and also in a considerable degree through the medium of the understanding.

Yorkshire General Meeting: A Sketch of the Origin, Progress and Present State of The Retreat ... pp. 10–11   Q

Most Friends today would oppose corporal punishment as inconsistent with our principles, though this
insight has emerged quite late in our history; Quakers
of an earlier generation often had little compunction
about it. I think that even today we can be a bit
priggish about it—there are many ways of being cruel
to a child, and a 'slap round the head' in anger can be
more honest and merciful than icy disapproval which
may last for days, with constant reminders of the
child's guilt, and no way out being offered. I always
believed that I should not hit my own children or
others for whom I was responsible. But I occasionally
did so, and the child understood and forgave
me—and at times even thought it was the right thing
for me to do. But where we go wrong is in justifying
ourselves, in building up a theory that it is right,
effective, for the child's good. The only justification
we should allow ourselves, in my opinion, is that of
the headmaster who said to me: 'When I cane a child,
it is because I don't know what to do: it is my confession that I have run out of constructive resources'.

I am not convinced by the people who say that
corporal punishment formed their character. 'I was
beaten every day as a child,' a prisoner told a friend of
mine, 'and it never did me any damage!' His conviction was for grievous bodily harm. Nor am I
impressed by the fact that many children say they
prefer it as a punishment. I suspect that it suits them
firstly because it is quickly over and done with, and
secondly because it allows you to end up feeling angry
if you want, instead of sorry. Compared to the effort of

* For retribution see *Exodus 21:12–25*; for restitution, *Exodus 22:1ff*. The logic of the two appears so similar until one realises that retribution does no one any actual good. See *Romans 12:17–21* on renouncing the right to revenge.

... It was decided to break the unit's long-standing prohibition against the use of corporal punishment (an almost universal rule in units dealing with mentally sick children). The agreement was that the very next time the boy spat in the face of anyone, that person should immediately hit the boy in the face. As luck would have it, my friend walked out of the meeting to be greeted by the offending child with the usual spit in the face. As agreed, he hit the boy. The result was dramatic. The boy was obviously both astonished and deeply upset by this unexpected violence from a gentle loving man—he never ever spat again. However, the consequence for the psychiatrist was equally marked; he was so disturbed by his own feelings in giving way to violence and to the recognition that part of him *wanted* to hit back in anger, that he realised he could never ever do that again.

Michael Rutter: *A Measure of our Values*, pp. 90–91   Q

putting things right, it is an 'easy way out'. Restitution* has also been called an easy option, but I have
not found it so, either for those who have to make
amends or for those who create opportunities for
them to do so. Consider how quickly you can break a
pane of glass, compared to the time needed to put
matters right by picking up the fragments, cleaning
out the frame, going to the glazier's, getting the new
piece cut, bringing it back and puttying it in. Which is
easier, to have 'six of the best', or to work for three
hours in the garden to earn enough to give one's
victim a treat at the cinema? When three boys at our
school who had bought drink illegally were sick on a
bus, they went for two successive Sunday mornings
to the depot to help clean out messed-up buses; and
they bought a piece of silk and made a batik scarf from
it for the woman sitting next to them. When they
appeared in court for the magistrates to adminster
retributive 'justice', they explained what they had
done. The magistrates told them that they had already
done more and better to put things to rights than
anything the court could have decided.

It is not my task here to convince you that we can
and should convert our criminal justice system into
one of restitution. But I think it is right for me to say
that as it stands it achieves so little good, and creates
so much evil, that we are called not to despair but to
work optimistically to transform it. Its answer to
deepest hurts in our society (at least, those of them
which we call crime) is imprisonment; and few of our
social institutions fall so short of their aims as this

While as Friends we are concerned to relate all aspects of social policy and practice to Christian principles, it is our conviction that the methods thus arising are also likely to be the most effective. Certainly our present systems and methods are increasingly ineffective, and seem to be rapidly approaching the point of breakdown. We believe that what is seen as a growing crisis in law and order has its roots in a fallacy, namely that where the majority are law-abiding, it is fear of punishment that deters people from crime. This has as its corollary the view that in times of increasing lawlessness, more punishment is the effective response.

Six Quakers Look at Crime and Punishment, p. 24   Q

2nd mo., 24th, 1818.—In the evening Martha Savory, my mother and I went to Newgate Gaol, where we met Elizabeth Fry, Peter Bedford and Edward Harris. We saw about fifteen poor men under sentence of death, who soon collected round us and stood with the most becoming and quiet attention, whilst my mother was engaged to preach the gospel of reconciliation . . . The two especially who had but a few hours to live, were encouraged to cast themselves upon the mercy and for-giveness of an all-gracious God whose power and goodness are the same as when they were manifested to the thief upon the cross . . . They wept freely, and though not able to *say* much, we fully believe they *felt*. It was difficult to tear our-selves from such a scene, and we turned from these poor sufferers under the feeling of indignant repugnance to the sanguinary nature of those laws which put so little value on human life, and adjudge punishments so disproportioned to, and so unlikely to prevent the renewal of crimes.

Elizabeth Dudley: *Memoirs*, p. 72   Q

does. Its first aim is to be a *deterrent*. The morality of deterrence can be questioned; but those of us who drive cars, for instance, must surely admit that deterrence does play a part in governing our driving habits. I went voluntarily into borstal several times when I was younger and learnt a great deal from my fellow-inmates; and more recently I have been close to two people who were imprisoned, one for arson and one for illicit sexual intercourse. In my limited experience I have found that the fear of the consequences was not present when the offence was committed. The arrest, remand and court appearances and the effect on friends and family, tended to have a powerful effect. One borstal boy said to me, 'If they let you home straight after that, you'd never do anything again!' I fear this is not true; but I do believe that the deterrent effect is at its greatest at that point, and that the rest of the time in prison, for many reasons, blunts that effect.

Imprisonment also offers some *protection* to society by removing the offender. But consider how limited that protection is compared to what it could be. It puts the offender against property into a place where he is deprived of opportunities to practice the social rules about property; it puts the violent man into a subculture which is governed by violence; it puts the defrauder into a power system where corruption is rife; it puts the sexual offender into a place where sexual relief is only obtainable by substitutes and perversions; it puts those who need to learn to take control of their lives into a situation where all signifi-

In the field of penal method, I may perhaps claim to speak with some measure of authority, having myself (as a Quaker 'war-resister') shared with many criminal offenders over twelve months of severe 'hard labour' sentences and afterwards helped to conduct a lengthy public enquiry into the penal system. The results of this enquiry played a considerable part in causing the prison authorities to abandon the regime, in force in British prisons up to about 1924, which definitely made retributive punishment the chief aim. It was shown fairly conclusively that this aim of retribution, however moral and 'majestic', could not be carried out without doing incalculable harm in most cases both to the prisoner and to the society of which he still remains a part, and often to those who administer his punishment.

Stephen Hobhouse: *Retribution and the Christian*,
p. 10   Q

As Friends, we believe in that of God in every human being. In our testimony based on the belief, we have also 'utterly denied all outward wars and strife and fighting with outward weapons' against those described as enemies of our country.

Implicit in these testimonies, we believe, is our repudiation of any right to humiliate, degrade or further damage those who are sometimes called the enemies of society, namely offenders.

Now as never before we need to protest at the harm being done to many of those caught up in the prison and criminal justice systems.

Friends' Penal Affairs Committee: *A Statement
of Conviction* (1981)   Q

* Note how Jesus does this, as reported in *Luke 7:36–50*.

72

cant choices are made for them; and it puts the
offender who is likely to reform into a *milieu* where
most of the influences on him or her are criminal ones.
It is small wonder that the many prison staff who
sincerely believe in *rehabilitation* (the third aim of
imprisonment) are continually disillusioned by their
impossible task, unless they are lucky enough to work
in one of the few special units. If we are sincerely and
intelligently concerned about the protection of
society, we must work to change a philosophy and
system which clearly increases the likelihood of
further crime when the prisoner is released.

This leaves the aim of *retribution*, about which I
have said enough. Just as institutionalisation is a perversion of true care, and compliance of reconciliation,
so I believe that retribution is the perversion of restitution. I will confess that, if you try consistently to
foster a system of making amends, you will be working at times with forced compliance. A convicted man
will agree to a community service order, or a child to
sweeping up the mess, because the alternative consequences are more fearsome. But this may be justi-
fied if the healing power of restitution is understood
and allowed to take effect. The job of putting things
right is often started grudgingly. But if there is inter-
est, support, actual help, praise, and in the end
approval and forgiveness, the initial feelings (born of
guilt and humiliation) are dissolved as the offender
finds that his efforts to show himself as good and
giving are recognised and he is welcomed back into
the human community.*

Portia:	Then must the Jew be merciful.
Shylock:	On what compulsion must I? Tell me that.
Portia:	The quality of mercy is not strained,

It droppeth as the gentle dew from heaven
Upon the earth beneath: it is twice blest,
It blesseth him that gives, and him that takes . . .
It is an attribute to God himself;
And earthly power does then prove most
    like God's
When mercy seasons justice. Therefore, Jew,
Though justice be thy plea, consider this,
That, in the course of justice, none of us
Should see salvation: we do pray for mercy,
And that same prayer doth teach us all to render
The deeds of mercy.

    William Shakespeare: *The Merchant of Venice*,
    Act IV, Scene 1

I remember a desperate and deprived boy who blindly got himself into one scrape after another. In school meetings he agreed to make amends, and older boys freely offered to help him. But he didn't turn up to do the things he had offered; if they found him and tried to persuade him, he became abusive or even violent. The list of uncompleted tasks grew, the willingness to help evaporated, and he became a scapegoat. In a meeting, someone mentioned one of the things he hadn't done, and the boy in charge of the meeting ordered him to go out and make a start. When he had gone, a member of staff brought up the whole situation. The boys pointed out how impossible it was to help him. Moreover he now had so much to do that he could not do it all even if he was willing; yet our trust in restitution depended on arrangements made in the meeting being carried out. 'The trouble is, he thinks we're all against him,' said a boy, 'how would it be if all of us set to together and got all these things done?' Many boys immediately offered, the people offended by John were satisfied, and his slate was clean. It was a turning point in his behaviour and relations with the community.

In '41 Mama took me back to Moscow. There I saw our enemies for the first time. If my memory is right, nearly 20,000 German war prisoners were to be marched in a single column through the streets of Moscow ... The crowd were mostly women— every one of them must have had a father or a husband, a brother or a son killed by the Germans . . . They were clenching their fists. The soldiers and policemen had all they could do to hold them back.

All at once something happened to them.

They saw German soldiers, thin, unshaven, wearing dirty blood-stained bandages, hobbling on crutches or leaning on the shoulders of their comrades; the soldiers walked with their heads down. The street became dead silent—the only sound was the shuffling of boots and the thumping of crutches.

Then I saw an elderly woman in broken-down boots push herself forward and touch a policeman's shoulder, saying: 'Let me through' ... She went up to the column, took from inside her coat something wrapped in a coloured handkerchief and unfolded it. It was a crust of black bread. She pushed it awk-wardly into the pocket of a soldier so exhausted that he was tottering on his feet. And now suddenly from every side women were running towards the soldiers, pushing into their hands bread, cigarettes, whatever they had.

The soldiers were no longer enemies. They were people.
Yevgeni Yevtushenko: *A Precocious Autobiography*, pp. 24–25

* This is emphasised in *Colossians 3:12–16*

Again and again I have walked to the tomb of a friendship, a working relationship, a love affair, with sweet spices in my hand, refusing to accept that there was no way I would be able to get in. We know, we women, we know all about earnestly desiring and waiting, about loving and suffering and going on anyway, witnesses to a different reality, a different way, an impossible possibility of resurrection.

Quaker Women's Group: *Bringing the Invisible into the Light*, p. 96   Q

Forgiveness

I have been talking about steps which we might take in the mending of hurts, steps which might lead to forgiveness. Though I have been thinking with you about people who cannot cope with their pain, I must stress the immense resources in each of us for healing and wholeness. This means that there are other ways to forgiveness besides the ones I have described. I think that cherishing, creative listening, reconciliation and restitution are among the most important. They also symbolise the different levels at which healing must take place. Though each of them works at several levels, and all of them are concerned with feelings, comfort and cherishing have important bodily aspects; creative listening is a spiritual discipline; reconciliation is concerned with the understanding; and both reconciliation and restitution involve social ideals.*

They are all deeply rooted in Quaker experience. Our form of worship and our belief in the divine element in everyone should teach us the skill and value of listening in the deepest way. We have a long history of work to relieve the victims of suffering, the mentally ill and those who have offended against the community. Out of these long-established concerns has grown the pioneer work of those Friends who have learnt special skills of reconciling those in conflict, and those who have challenged the concept of retribution by developing opportunities for restitu-

'You shall not nurse hatred against your brother. You shall reprove your fellow-countryman frankly and for that you will incur no blame. You shall not seek revenge, or cherish anger towards your kinsfolk; you shall love your neighbour as a man like yourself. I am the Lord.' *Leviticus 19:18*

This idea acquires further expression within the laws regarding the Day of Atonement, in the teaching that 'The Day of Atonement can only atone for sins between humans and God, but sins between people can only be atoned for by asking one's fellow for forgiveness and appeasing him/her directly.' (In typical Jewish fashion, every consequence has to be spoken for, and thus 'if one has asked for forgiveness sincerely three times and the offended person still refuses to grant it, then God forgives the petitioner and the other becomes the sinner for his/her hardheartedness'!)

Rabbi David Rosen

But this imperfectly-taught woman, whose phrases and habits were an odd patchwork, had a loyal spirit within her. The man whose prosperity she had shared through nearly half a life and who had unvaryingly cherished her—now that punishment had befallen him it was not possible to her in any sense to forsake him. There is a forsaking which still sits at the same board and lies on the same couch with the forsaken soul, withering it the more by unloving proximity. She knew, when she locked the door, that she should unlock it ready to go down to her unhappy husband and espouse his sorrow, and say of his guilt, I will mourn and not reproach. But she needed time to gather up her strength; she needed to sob out her farewell to all the gladness and pride of her life.

George Eliot: *Middlemarch*,
Book VIII Chapter lxxiv

* Consider the experience of the paralysed man told in *Mark* 2:1–12

tion. We cannot take to ourselves the full credit for this still-growing tradition, but we can recognise its worth and that we each may be called to play a part in developing it.

All pain calls for healing; but we talk about forgiveness in connection with the pain we cause each other, what I have been describing as 'hurts'. There are different ways to reach it, but I am convinced that without forgiveness hurts are not healed. It has two aspects, forgiving and being forgiven, and both are needed. Until we forgive, pain persists; until we are forgiven, guilt remains. All too often, there is mutual wrong, and both parties need both to give and receive forgiveness.

Both giving it and receiving it can be difficult. Some people have the grace for forgiving readily and generously, while others find it costly, and perhaps can only do it little by little. I do not pretend I can explain these differences, still less pass judgement that the one is 'better' or 'worse' that the other. It is wiser to see the power to forgive as God's gift to us, given perhaps at the moment when we feel: 'I have a right to my anger and bitterness; but I begin to see that it is a burden as well as a right. Lord, I feel helpless; what can I do?' Both prayer and spiritual healing play a part in this process*—two subjects which are close to the theme of this lecture, but I do not have the experiences and insights from which to enlarge on them.

You may hear someone say, 'She forgave him, but he can't forgive himself.' But I wonder if we can ever forgive ourselves? We have an accuser inside us who

Forgiveness is unconditional or it is not forgiveness at all. Forgiveness has the character of 'in spite of', but the righteous ones give it the character of 'because'. The sinners however cannot do this. They cannot transform the divine 'in spite of' into a human 'because'. They cannot show facts, because of which they must be forgiven . . . God's forgiveness is independent of anything we do, even of self-accusation and self-humilation. If this were not so, how could we ever be certain that our self-rejection is serious enough to deserve forgiveness? Forgiveness creates repentance—this is declared in our story [of the woman in the house of Simon the Pharisee, *Luke 7:36–50*] and this is the experience of those who have been forgiven . . .

In the minds of many people the word 'forgiveness' has connotations which completely contradict the way Jesus deals with the woman in our story. Many of us think of solemn acts of pardon, of release from punishment, in other words, of another act of righteousness by the righteous ones. But genuine forgiveness is participation, reunion overcoming the powers of estrangement. And only because this is so, does forgiveness make love possible. We cannot love unless we have accepted forgiveness, and the deeper our experience of forgiveness is, the greater is our love. We cannot love where we feel rejected, even if the rejection is done in righteousness.

Paul Tillich: *The Boundaries of our Being*, pp. 157-59

Your sins are forgiven: that is to say, you are reunited with the reality of which you are a part, as soon as you see what is really happening. When you do, you will forgive others. If you can't, it's an indication that you haven't really seen the way things are.

Sydney Carter: *The Rock of Doubt*, § 13
(This is the point of the story in *Matthew 18:23–35*)

speaks with a voice not ours: whether it is the Freud-ian superego, the social conscience, or God, or the devil. (The word 'devil' means accuser, and Satan in The Book of Job is described as one of the Sons of God.) When the voice of this accuser falls silent, we feel at peace. But we cannot still it ourselves—and the cost of deafening ourselves to it is too high. And yet the teaching of the gospels is that God's forgiveness is always there, waiting for us. We can accept it, though we can do nothing to earn it; but we can only receive it if we are willing to let it change us.

Forgiveness, human and divine, looks forward. It is the means whereby the future can be different from the past. It is not the same as resignation or acceptance because of this element of hope; it believes that things can change. This means that there is no forgiveness except when we are willing ourselves to change. To say 'I forgive you (or, I am forgiven) but it makes no difference' is self-contradictory. The logic of forgiveness, of reconciliation, is not compatible with the logics of cynicism and cruelty and selfish-ness. These too are rational patterns of behaviour—though we may also see them as evidence that their practitioners have hidden wounds. But when we choose forgiveness we must see clearly that it is an alternative to these other logics; they cannot co-exist in us.

In speaking to you from my own experience, I have been drawing on personal encounters. Forgiveness too only has meaning as a personal thing. So what hope can we offer for the hurts felt by whole groups of

From a Teviot Tower flat in Newtown, Birmingham, race relations is a pressing social issue, vital in its consequences for all residents, and craving the attention of politicians and policy makers. From a four-bedroomed, £90,000 house in Sir Harry's Road, Edgbaston, race relations is little more than a media invention. 'It's all been blown up, especially lately,' Stanley Mills insists, 'There's a lot of hypocrisy about today with the media and do-gooders carrying on about coloureds. I think you create a problem where there isn't one by drawing attention to it. Things aren't too bad at the moment.'

E. Ellis Cashmore: 'Who are the real racists?'
New Society 13 June 1986.

Half of him, a deep, instinctive, natural, impulsive half wanted to go back [into the condemned cell], clasp Hara in his arms, kiss him goodbye on the forehead and say: 'We may not be able to stop and undo the hard old wrongs of the great world outside, but through you and me no evil shall come, either in the unknown where you are going, or in the imperfect and haunted dimension of awareness through which I move. Thus, between us, we shall cancel out all private and personal evil, thus arrest private and personal consequences to blind action and reaction, thus prevent specifically the general incomprehension and misunderstanding, hatred and revenge of our time from spreading further.' But the words would not be uttered, and half of him, the conscious half of the officer at the door with a critical, alert sentry at his side, held him powerless on the threshold.

Laurens van der Post: *The Sower and the Seed*, p.36

people, the oppressed and those who are showing their anger?

When we look at their problems, we see—if we are honest—that the large-scale problem is mirrored in each one of us. If we consider young black people in English cities, we can see the failure to care, the economic factors, the creation of ghettos, the social deprivation, and the way that they hurt one another by drugs, vandalism and crimes. We feel that the authorities should do something about it. But we do not seriously want to alter our personal economic situation to help them; we do not want to end the ghettos by living with them, or they with us; we do not want to take the risk that we might have to share the burden of the drugs and crime problems. So the problem is inside us as well as out there.

We can also see that the victims carry the pain inside them as individuals as well as in a group. The long-standing neglect of the Catholic community where I live, in Derry, took the particular form that there was much more work for women (of a low-paid and oppressive sort) than for men, though the culture promoted masculine superiority. In housing estates where four or six able-bodied men in ten were unemployed, how was the individual man to assert his virility? For many, the means were hard drinking and begetting lots of children. All too often, they added violence directed at their wives and children to assert themselves and maintain the illusion of being in control. In recent years, paramilitary violence gave a further option. We can see how injustice to a whole

There is so much for us all to forgive that we shall never get it done without putting in a lot of practice. Every act of forgiveness is a raid on the kingdom of fear.

Neville Ward: *Five for Sorrow, Ten for Joy*, p. 52

* From Laurens van der Post: *The Sower and the Seed*, p. 37.

The world which I had condemned did no more than remind me of its existence by causing me to suffer. And what was this world—a multitude in chaos, an ordered multitude, a single being, a whole? What were the feathers on the arrow, heron or jay? What was the poison on its tip, snake-venom or plant? Knowledge alone could not create an acceptable bond between me and the world; it could only show the world to be alien and indifferent, the source of pain. I could hate it easily enough, but I had never tried to love it. That was less easy. Did not everything that had happened to me and everything I had done go to prove that knowledge and experience could only bring me hatred and fear of the world and I must try something else? Did they not show that the world itself was impelling me through suffering towards a course that I should otherwise not have contemplated—the effort to love and forgive it? But since I was part of the world, with everything that I was and did, then my love and forgiveness were the world's own love and forgiveness, which it was teaching me in this harsh fashion, the only one I was capable of understanding. And if to love and forgive the world could bring me comfort and joy, was not this the proof of its own love and forgiveness? Whence did I acquire the power to love and forgive except from the world, from life itself, which had bestowed it on me, ready for my use when I was ready to use it?

Petru Dumitriu: *Incognito*, p. 354

group was felt in the individual man (and in each woman too in other ways), and how his personal need to respond in some way increased the problems of the whole group.

So the hurt owned by the group is felt by the individual. And though I respect the work of those who are trying to build institutions for a more just and peaceful world and society, I do not myself know anywhere that hurts can be mended except in me and you and her and him. 'Was not that how great things began, in the tiny seed of the small change in the troubled individual heart?' asks Laurens van der Post; 'one single, lonely, inexperienced heart had to change first, and all the rest would follow?'* So often we are guided to action which is small, ridiculous against the scale of our concern. If we obey, we will be judged as religious fanatics. But if our faith is weak, we can also take hope from the work of the systems theorists, who study the processes of change. They tell us that if you introduce new information into a system, if you alter your patterns of response, you inevitably change it.

On Good Friday in 1985, a large wooden cross was carried to the square in front of the Guildhall in Derry. Beneath its shadow, Northern Irish Roman Catholics and Protestants and a group from England in turn confessed the wrongs which their people had done to the others represented there, and forgave one another. The act of repentance and forgiveness starts in the individual; but who knows where it ends?

Throughout 1976 eyewitnesses spoke of unprovoked shoot-
ings in the townships, directed not at crowds but individuals
... Children too young to know what was happening were
gunned down in the streets. In Cape Town in September,
Sandra Peters, aged 11, was shot through the head as she went
shopping for her grandmother. When her mother went to
inquire what had happened, she was arrested and kept in
custody. Two days later Sandra died in hospital ... One victim
was an 8-year-old girl who innocently raised her fist in a *black
power* salute as a Hippo [troop carrier] passed. 'The Hippo
stopped and opened fire on that child. On the Saturday we
went to the mortuary and found the body of the little girl
riddled with bullets.'

I.D.A.F.: *Children Under Apartheid*, p. 96

From today on, Dear Diary, we're not in a ghetto but a ghetto-
camp, and on every house they've pasted a notice which tells
exactly what we're not allowed to do ... Actually everything is
forbidden, but the most awful thing of all is that the punishment for everything is death. There is no difference between
things; no standing in the corner, no spankings, no taking
away food, no writing down the declensions of irregular verbs
a hundred times, the way it used to be in school. Not at all—the
lightest and the heaviest punishment is death. It doesn't actually say that this punishment also applies to children, but I
think it does apply to us too.

Eva Heyman (aged 13): *Diary*, entry for 10 May, 1944

Sacrifice

It would be comforting to end there; but it would not be honest. For we know of wrongs so monstrous that it seems like a travesty even to talk of forgiveness. This is expressed, better than I could, in a famous passage of *The Brothers Karamazov*:

> If the sufferings of children go to make up the sum of sufferings which is necessary for the purchase of truth, then I say beforehand that the entire truth is not worth such a price. I do not want a mother to embrace the torturer who had her child torn to pieces by dogs! She has no right to forgive him. If she likes, she can forgive him for herself, she can forgive the torturer for the immeasurable suffering he has inflicted on her as a mother; but she has no right to forgive him for the sufferings of her tortured child. She has no right to forgive the torturer for that, even if her child were to forgive him! And if that is so, what becomes of the harmony? . . . I don't want harmony, I don't want it, out of the love I bear to mankind. I want to remain with my suffering unavenged. I'd rather remain with my suffering unavenged and my indignation unappeased, *even*

* Quotation opposite from Fyodor Dostovevsky: *The Brothers Karamazov* Book V chapter 4: 'Rebellion'. See also Ursula Le Guin's short story, 'Those who walk away from Omelas.'

There are two forces in our battered world. One is the force of those who, like the suffering servant of God, exist, unseen, in all countries. We do not know where these servants live, or what they will make of the future. But we know that they exist, and that their suffering is not vain. They are the hidden tools of the God of history. They are the aged and the children, the young men and the young women, the persecuted and the imprisoned, and all those sacrificed for the sake of the future, for one small stone in the building of the Kingdom of God, the cornerstone of which is the perfect Servant of God. And the second force of the world is the force of those who, like Cyrus, rule empires, and incorporate all the shame and greatness of empires. They are the men of God's counsel, because they carry through his purposes in the service of the suffering servants of Jahweh. But they are not aware that they are instruments . . .

Paul Tillich: *The Shaking of the Foundations*, p. 40

* For Danilo Dolci, see James McNeish: *Fire Under the Ashes*, chapters 4–6

if I were wrong. Besides, too high a price has been placed on harmony. We cannot afford to pay so much for admission ... It's not God that I do not accept, Alyosha. I merely most respectfully return him the ticket.*

In a little fishing village called Trappetto in Sicily, in 1954, a girl called Giustina Barretta had a baby in a one-room house with a sewer flowing past the door. Her milk dried up from starvation, and a few days later she and Danilo Dolci watched while the baby died. Not long after, torn by this and other experiences, Danilo had a few copies made of a letter in which he said that he would not eat again unless the village was given help and the opportunity of work. He lay down in that same room and waited. The letters were sent off almost at random, and no one in authority took any notice. The woman of the village could not understand what he was doing; they thought he must have made some sort of vow to the Madonna. They brought such food as they could, and begged him to eat. The parish priest was not to be seen throughout the fast. A few of the fishermen, more in desperation than hope, supported him and decided that, when he died, one of them would take his place.

In human terms, Danilo could see no way forward.* His action contained, perhaps, an element of despair—that there was no reason or no right to stay alive in a world which allowed the injustice of the baby's death. There was too an element of faith, an

Pure wisdom leads people into lowliness of mind, in which they will learn resignation to the divine Will, and contentment in suffering for his cause, when they cannot keep a clear conscience without suffering.

John Woolman: *Considerations on Pure Wisdom and Human Policy*, p. 1   Q

It was the start of a bitter winter.
The soldiers' violence continued.
     Sleepless nights of horrendous noise
     and searchlights
               Frightened children
     Bricks and stones thrown
     and verbal rape of obscene language.
So we came to the *violet gate*
bruised and cold and vilified.
We came to the violet gate of sacrifice.
We had thought it enough to leave the known
and take the way of the unknown
but this we did not expect.

What is to give light must endure the burning.

Tony Biggin and others: *The Gates of Greenham.*   Q

* Quoted from *Psalm 50*

absurd trust that if he offered everything, without hope, the world would change. And there was an element of sacrifice.

Sacrifice, a concept which pervades the bible, makes us uncomfortable. There is first the horror of it, the skull-rack of ancient Mexico, the tabernacle of Jehovah splashed with warm animal blood. Then there is the aspect of the too-easy way out of guilt. When Prometheus first offered sacrifice to Zeus, he is said to have hidden the good meat in the animal's stomach, and wrapped the fat and the bones in the handsome skin. Zeus was asked to decide which portion would fall to the gods, and which to men; he chose the skin, and was furious when he discovered its paltry contents. This legend expresses our feeling that in sacrifice men offer God a second-best, to save themselves. Even the concept of self-sacrifice may seem, in the actions of some Christian saints, to have a strong taint of masochism. And the contemplation of the crucifixion itself has at times become an unholy obsession with the details of *someone else's* suffering. And we are not helped to understand it by our modern tendency to describe every little renunciation or discomfort as a sacrifice. We are tempted to dismiss the whole idea with the magnificent words which the psalmist puts into God's mouth: 'If I be hungry, I will not tell you; for everything in the world is mine . . .'*

Yet when we think of the bombs at Hiroshima and Nagasaki, or 'the final solution of the Jewish Problem', we are confronting evil which our reason cannot

So I can perceive that it requires strength and energy and freedom of spirit to make the infinite movement of resignation. I can also perceive that it is feasible. But the next thing astonishes me, it makes my head swim, for after having made the movement of resignation, then by virtue of the absurd to get everything, to get the wish whole and uncurtailed—that is beyond human power, it is a prodigy . . . and yet this movement is the movement of faith, and remains such even though philosophy in order to confuse the concepts would make us believe that it has faith, and even though theology would sell out faith at a bargain price.

Søren Kierkegaard: Fear and Trembling, p. 58

* Jesus' words quoted from *Luke, 9:23–24*.

Easter 1960. Forgiveness breaks the chain of causality because he who 'forgives' you—out of love—takes upon himself the consequences of what *you* have done. Forgiveness therefore always entails a sacrifice.

The price you must pay for your own liberation through another's sacrifice, is that you in turn must be willing to liberate in the same way, irrespective of the consequences to yourself.

Dag Hammarskjöld: Markings, p. 163

grasp, which is too vast for our usual emotional reactions. We are reduced to silence, terror and awe. Some Jewish thinkers speak of the times when God hides his face; his ordering power seems to be withdrawn, and the vessels which hold it broken. But that of God in us persists; it remains to take the full attack of the forces of evil in the disordered world.

Danilo offered his life. And, miraculously, by a series of chances, his cry was heard and the Italian government responded with the help which the village needed. His despair was turned into power. The solution came from beyond him; but it came through his *accepting responsibility*. In his case, we can see how his offer of himself changed things. But it is in the nature of sacrifice that we cannot always know its workings or see its results.

Jesus said, 'If any man will come after me, let him deny himself, and take up his cross daily, and follow me. For whosoever will save his life shall lose it; but whosoever will lose his life for my sake, the same shall save it.'* These are frightening words. But they contain a seed of hope. In the ongoing cycles of wrong and counter-wrong, hurt and retaliation, which we have thought about, we are both victims and assassins. We are wounded, and at the same time we bear the blood, the pain, of others on our hands. The sacrifice which each of us can make is to say, 'The hurt which my sister or brother is causing me is born of the wounds which all of us have given them. And in hurting them, we were reacting to other hurts, some from the distant past. Who knows how far this par-

93

His Power was made manifest and his Word spoke within me, which Word was in my heart, and was as a fire or a hammer . . . And by this Word was I called to forsake father and mother, lands and living, to go in obedience to the Lord who commanded me not to take thought what I should eat, or what I should drink, or wherewith I should be clothed, but cast my care upon him.

> Richard Hubberthorne: *A True Testimony of Obedience*, pp. 1–2.   Q

My dear friend,

I now feel in a good degree easy about my dear little motherless children . . . I have now given them up to God, and their and my friends . . . and whatever becomes of me, my soul at present in tenderness and prostration bows before the throne of grace on their account; and craves almighty aid and the watchful guardianship of their friends for them. I may again have them under my immediate care or I never may. God only knows; and to him I commit myself and them, and rest thy friend, J.S.

> Job Scott: Letter in *Journal*, 21, 1st mo., 1792   Q

Christ Jesus, the Immanuel, (of whose sufferings the scriptures declare) him alone I confess before men; for whose sake I have denied whatever was dear to me in this world, that I might win him and be found in him and not in myself . . . , that in me he may be glorified, whether by life or death; and for his sake I suffer all things, that he alone may have the glory of my change, whose work alone it is in me.

James Naylor: 'A Testimony to Christ Jesus, delivered to the Parliament who persecuted him as a blasphemer: written in the time of his imprisonment in Bridewell.' *Collected Works*

> p. xxxv   Q

ticular chain goes back, binding us together in a dark prison of revenge and pain? But I am resolved that what I now carry will not be passed on. No one else will have cause to stumble under its weight, because I accept this suffering, and will it to end in me.'

I believe that most of us are called to make this sacrifice at some time or other. We may be caught up in events which make the choice inescapable, as Friends are in South Africa today. Or the Word of God may resonate in us till, like Richard Hubberthorne or Daniel Wheeler, we set out on a great adventure. But this stride of soul is as huge when we choose to take it in our own familiar place.

To offer up to God our right to feel angry, our ownership of our pain, may seem a very small step— perhaps just the forgiving of a careless word. But it is a step on a path that may lead to lonely and terrible places: to the Boston quay where Job Scott embarked on his journey 'in the ministry' to Europe, after he had said goodbye to his motherless children, with a presentment that he would not return alive from Europe; to the scaffold where James Naylor kissed the executioner who was about to bore through his tongue; to the Pentagon steps where our fellow-Quaker, Norman Morrison, burnt himself to death during the napalm bombing of Vietnam. Such actions appal us, and it is right that they should. Any other reaction is quite inappropriate—particularly the embarrassment which Friends felt about James Naylor for nearly three hundred years, and which it seems we now feel about Norman Morrison. And yet, when we are confronted

NORMAN MORRISON

On November 2nd 1965
in the multi-coloured, multi-minded
United beautiful States of terrible America
Norman Morrison set himself on fire
outside the Pentagon.
He was thirty-one, he was a Quaker,
and his wife (seen weeping in the newsreels)
and his three children
survive him as best they can.
He did it in Washington where everyone could see
because
people were being set on fire
in the dark corners of Vietnam where nobody could see.
Their names, ages, beliefs and loves
are not recorded.
This is what Norman Morrison did.
He poured petrol over himself.
He burned. He suffered.
He died.
That is what he did
in the white heart of Washington
where everyone could see.
He simply burnt away his clothes,
his passport, his pink-tinted skin,
put on a new skin of flame
and became
Vietnamese.

Adrian Mitchell

*Quotation opposite from T. S. Eliot: *The Waste Land*, part V.

with hurt to ourselves or others, and the rational ways of mending it are not effective, we are forced to choose between complicity in the universal wrong and an act of sacrifice. Then the divine voice inside us insists that this is the most important choice of all.

> . . . What have we given?
> My friend, blood shaking my heart,
> The awful daring of a moment's surrender
> Which an age of prudence can never retract,
> By this, and this only, we have existed . . .*

This choice is no less important when it takes place in secret, among the daily knocks and disappointments of what is called a humdrum life. It is easier for me to call those witnesses whose sacrifices took place on a public stage; but I am talking about something which does not usually demand long journeys, dramatic renunciations, or heroic endurance, in the sense that the people around us will recognise. The journey, the renunciation, the heroism, may be called for within our own hearts, a private matter between us and God.

It happens when we accept the hurt, and do not let it enslave or degrade us, but endure it, and refuse to pass it on. When we choose this path, we cannot forsee its end; we can't say if it will do any good. It is a starting point, not a solution. We don't know what will be asked of us next. But by this sacrifice we have identified ourselves with whatever power there is in the universe to redeem and recreate. After his suffering (not the least of which was his rejection by his

Mother could not help smiling at that. She wept and smiled at the same time. 'How are you,' she said, 'most of all responsible for everyone? There are murderers and robbers in the world, and what terrible sin have you committed that you should accuse yourself before everyone else?' 'Mother, my dearest heart,' said my brother (he had begun using such caressing, such unexpected words just then), 'my dearest heart, my joy, you must realise that everyone is really responsible for everyone and everything. I don't know how to explain it to you, but I feel it so strongly that it hurts. And how could we have gone on living and getting angry without knowing anything about it?' ... 'Your son hasn't long to live,' the doctor said to my mother, when she saw him off at the front door, 'I'm afraid his illness is affecting his brain.'

Fyodor Dostoyevsky: *The Brothers Karamazov*, Book VI chapter 2(a)

* Quotation from James Naylor: Epistle XI *Collected Works*, p. 729

† This concept of the crucifixion is foreshadowed in *Isaiah 53* and discussed in my *Twenty Questions about Jesus* (Question 16).

God's plan for the ultimate defeat of pain, suffering and tragedy is clear. It does not involve duelling it to the ground. It doesn't mean staying clear of its grasp. It doesn't mean searching out and destroying all the strongholds of evil in others that would cause or precipitate pain. God's plan is to enter into the middle of pain and suffering and *there* break its power by transcending it. To break its grinding horror from the inside out. The incarnation did exactly that. God entered into the horror of human existence and there lived out an alternative, and through the atonement made it possible that each of us can do the same.

Jan Wood: *Talk at World Gathering of Young Friends*, 1985   Q

brother- and sister-Quakers), James Naylor wrote of this Seed, 'who seeks not revenge, but endures all contradictions from all against himself, to the end he may obtain mercy for all from the Father. And this is the Seed of eternal peace, and the eternal Peace-maker, which . . . hath power to endure all things, and subdue all things by overcoming.'* Freedom, and joy, may be the unexpected harvest.

We come together because a young man, nearly two thousand years ago, took this road. We argue now about who he was, or how we should interpret the records of him. Whatever is obscure, we can see one thing clearly.† The other actors in the drama of his death were caught in those chains of guilt, hate and violence: Jewish humiliation, Roman imperialism; the police used for repressive purposes; the priests corrupted by political aims; Judas the Dagger-man (or terrorist), the other disciples who ran away in panic. Jesus refused to let Peter fight; he refused to call on the angels who, he believed, were standing by. He would not forge the next link in the chain of hurt and revenge. He allowed all those others to crush him with their pain and hate, unresisting, forgiving, trusting that he could take all their evil into himself and so bring it to an end.

A Song of Pain and Anger

Words & Music: John Lampen

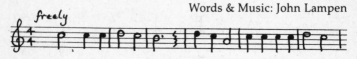

1,4 Lost in an endless sea (1) all alone, In the bitter tasting
(4) once again,

wind, and the thrill of the cold runs through me, Clinging to my

rock with two bare hands.　2. Now I see the fac-es laugh
3. So the embers of the past

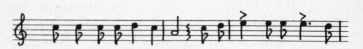

Feel the bruises on my back, Hear the crowd of my mem-ories
Break a-gain to scorching fire, But the flames cannot melt the

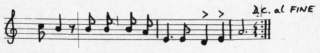

screaming, Screaming in the voices which I loved.
pri-son, Of the walls of ice around my heart.

100

A Song of Forgiveness

Words & Music: John Lampen

I saw him standing in the eve-ning light; I tried to pass, pre-

-tended not to see. He picked the one re - maining apple from the

tree, and offered it to me.

I put my load aside, reached out my hand;
I felt the tears run down my dirty cheek.
He drew me from the path, we sat down side by side,
    And found we could not speak.

The end of day, the trees, the dusty road,
And one lone bird gave thanks for him and me.
The night no longer threatened loneliness and hate,
    But peace and mystery.

Resources

The contraints on a lecturer have meant that many themes and issues could only be briefly explored or referred to; many of the books quoted can be used as resources for further enquiry, but those listed below have been particularly helpful to me.

Comfort and Cherishing

THOMAS Liz: *Dust of Life*. Hamish Hamilton, 1977 — memoir.
CROMPTON Margaret: *Respecting Children*. Arnold, 1980.
TAYLOR Michael: *Learning to Care*. SPCK, 1983.

Working with the Pain

HOBSON, R. H. *Forms of Feeling: The Heart of Psychotherapy*. Tavistock, 1986.
JACOBS Michael: *Swift to Hear*. SPCK, 1985.
LAMPEN Diana: *Facing Death*. QHS, 1979 — the process of "working through" pain.
PINNEY Rachel: *Creative Listening*. Privately printed; London 1981.
SANDFORD Agnes: *The Healing Light*. Arthur James, 1978 — spiritual healing.

Reconciliation

AUGSBURGER David: *When Caring is not Enough: resolving conflicts through fair fighting*. Herald Press, 1983.
BEER Jennifer: *Peacemaking in Your Neighbourhood*. Friends' Suburban Project, Philadelphia, 1982.
BLATTNER Howard: *Acting-In*. Springer, USA, 1973 — psychodrama.

CURLE Adam: *In the Middle: non-official mediation in violent situations.* Berg, 1986.

FISHER William & URY Roger: *Getting to Yes.* Hutchinson, 1986.

KRAYBILL Ron: *Repairing the Breach.* Mennonite Central Committee, USA, 1981.

MOORE Christopher: *The Mediation Process.* California, Jossey-Bass, 1986.

MURDOCH Iris: *A Word Child.* Penguin, 1986 — novel.

Restitution

ALCOHOLICS ANONYMOUS: *Twelve Steps and Twelve Traditions.* London, 1980.

DOSTOYEVSKY Fyodor: *Crime & Punishment.* Novel — various translations available.

HOBHOUSE, Stephen: *Retribution and the Christian.* Fellowship of Reconciliation, 1942.

Six Quakers Look at Crime and Punishment. QHS, 1979.

SPELLER Adrian: *Breaking Out; A Christian Critique of Criminal Justice.* Hodder, 1986.

WILLS David: *Throw Away Thy Rod.* Gollancz, 1960.

Forgiveness

DUMITRIU Petru: *Incognito* tr. Norman Denny. Collins, 1964 — novel.

TILLICH Paul: *The Boundaries of Our Being.* Fontana, 1973.

Sacrifice

BRINK Andre: *A Dry White Season.* Fontana, 1984 — novel.

HAMMARSKJOLD Dag: *Markings* tr. W. H. Auden & Leif Sjoberg. Faber, 1966.

KELLY Thomas: *A Testament of Devotion.* QHS, 1979.

Books quoted

List of titles quoted and referred to; the page numbers beneath each quotation are from the edition or translation given below. In some instances permission to include an extract had to be obtained from the publisher of the original edition. These publishers are given in brackets. The author and Quaker Home Service gladly make acknowledgement to all the writers and publishers for their permission to quote from copyright sources.

Page no.
of text

AUDEN, W. H. *In Memory of Sigmund Freud.* 1939, in various anthologies.   10

BIGGIN Tony, and others: *The Gates of Greenham,* Leaveners Press, 1985.   90

BOESAK Alan: *The Finger of God* tr. Peter Randal. New York: Orbis, 1982.   46

BONNHOEFFER Dietrich: *The Cost of Discipleship.* Translated by R. H. FULLER. SCM, 1959.   64

BRITTAIN Vera: *Testament of Youth.* Virago, 1978.   12

CARDENAL Ernesto: *Psalms* tr. John Griffiths & others. Sheed & Ward, 1981 (Search Press).   2

CARTER Sydney: *The Rock of Doubt.* Mowbrays, 1978.   80

CASHMORE, E. Ellis: 'Who are the real racists?' in New Society, 13 June, 1986.   82

CRAIG Mary: *Blessings.* Hodder & Stoughton, 1979.   2

CRESSWELL Mrs Francis: *A Memoir of Elizabeth Fry.* London, 1868.   24

CURLE Adam: *True Justice.* QHS, 1981.   36

DENNING Lord: *Evidence to the Royal Commission on Capital Punishment,* 1953.   52

McNEISH James: *Fire under the Ashes* [Danilo Dolci]. Hodder & Stoughton, 1965. 88

MANDELSTAM Nadeshda: *Hope Abandoned* tr. Max Hayward. Penguin, 1976 (Collins/Harvill, 1974). 58

MITCHELL Adrian: 'Norman Morrison' in *Outloud*. Cape, 1964. 96

MURDOCH Iris: *Bruno's Dream*. Penguin, 1970 (Chatto & Windus,1969). 6

NAYLOR James: *Collected Works*. London, 1716. 94, 99

PARKER Alexander: Letter to Margaret Fell 15.6.1658 in *Letters of Early Friends*. London, 1841. 54

PARKER Tony & ALLERTON Robert: *The Courage of his Convictions*. Century Hutchinson, 1962. 22

PENINGTON Isaac: *Collected Works*. Second Edn., London, 1761. 60

QUAKER WOMEN'S GROUP: *Bringing the Invisible into the Light*. QHS, 1986. 76

ROSEN David: personal communication. 78

RUTTER Michael: *A Measure of Our Values*. QHS, 1983. 68

SCOTT Job: *Journal*. London, 1843. 94

SEFERIS George: 'Gymnopaedia' in *Collected Poems* translated and edited by Edmund Keely and Philip Sherrard. Cape, 1969. 4

SHAKESPEARE William: *King Lear* viii
Macbeth 28
The Merchant of Venice. 74

SHEFF David: *The Playboy Interviews* with John Lennon and Yoko Ono. New English Library, 1982. 4

Six Quakers Look at Crime and Punishment. QHS, 1979. 36, 70

STACEY Nicholas: quoted in *The Listener*, 6 February, 1986.   18

TILLICH Paul: *The Boundaries of Our Being*. Fontana, 1973 (*The Eternal Now*, SCM, 1963 and *The New Being*, SCM, 1956).   28, 80
The Shaking of the Foundations. Penguin, 1972 (SCM).   88

TOURNIER Paul: *The Violence Inside* tr. Eward Hudson. SCM, 1978.   42

ULLMAN Richard: *Dilemmas of a Reconciler*. QPS, 1984.   44

VAN DER POST Laurens: *The Seed and the Sower*. Penguin, 1966 (Hogarth Press,1965).   82, 85

VANIER Jean: *Be Not Afraid*. Gill & Macmillan, 1975.   14

WARD Neville: *Five for Sorrow, Ten for Joy*. Epworth, 1971.   84

WARREN Will: Talk to IFoR 1977 see *Will Warren: A Scrapbook*, QHS, 1983.   58

WILLS David: *The Barns Experiment*. Allen & Unwin, 1945.   62

WILSON Roger: *Quaker Relief*. Allen & Unwin, 1952.   16

WINNICOTT Donald: *Playing and Reality*. Penguin, 1974 (Tavistock Pubs, 1971).   24

WOOD Jan: Talk to World Gathering of Young Friends in *Let Your Lives Speak*, WGYF, 1986.   98

WOOLMAN John: *Journal*. Various editions available   54
Considerations on Pure Wisdom and Human Policy. London, 1773.   90

WORLD GATHERING OF YOUNG FRIENDS: Epistle   10
Talk by Jan Wood, both in *Let Your Lives Speak*, WGYF, 1986.   98

YARROW Mike: *Quaker Experiences in International Reconciliation*. Yale, 1978.   44

YEVTUSHENKO Yevyeni: *A Precocious Autobiography*
  tr. A. R. MacAndrew. Collins & Harvill, 1963   76
YORKSHIRE GENERAL MEETING: *A Sketch of the
  Origin, Progress, and Present State of
  The Retreat*. York, 1828   66

Bible references

THE SWARTHMORE LECTURES

The following lectures have been reprinted in
different formats.

Several of the Lectures earlier than 1975 are still in print and a
complete list will be sent on request to Quaker Home Service,
Friends House, Euston Road, London NW1 2BJ.